THE MAN'S SECRET

TO A HAPPY AND SEXY MARRIAGE

in less than
10 minutes
a day

THE **MAN'S SECRET** TO A **HAPPY** AND **SEXY MARRIAGE**

in less than **10 minutes** a day

Steve Schloss

MANTOMANTALKS
M E D I A
PRINCETON

Published by: Man To Man Talks Media
www.mantomantalks.com
Printed in the United States of America
Illustrations Copyright © 2013 by Anthea Margot
Cover design by Kathi Dunn, www.dunn-design.com
Interior Design by Anthea Margot
Author Photography by Anthea Margot
Library of Congress Cataloging-in-Publication Data
Schloss, Steve.
The Man's Secret ™ to a Happy and Sexy Marriage in Less Than 10 Minutes a Day
Steve Schloss— 1ˢᵗ Edition
ISBN-13:
978-0615793825 (Man To Man Talks Media)
ISBN-10:
0615793827

DEDICATION

This book has been a labor of love and is dedicated to the following:

To my awesome children Niki and Dan; remember that health and happiness are the most important things in life. I love you guys so much!

To my parents, Myra and Morton Schloss, who have been happily married for 70 years. You have set an excellent example of dedication toward each other and within your marriage.

In Loving Memory to Michael Schwartz, my brother-in-law and husband to my sister Debbie. Mike was a testimony of how to be a *wonderful* husband. Every night when he came home from work, Mike would passionately and actively listen to Debbie talk about her day. This is when I first recognized that the simple things in life are the foundation for a happy marriage.

I also dedicate this book to all the unhappily married men in the world. May you find solutions that rejuvenate the love and passion like the day you first married your wife.

CONTENTS

CONTENTS

.....AND DO YOU PROMISE TO LOVE, HONOR AND
PLEAD FOR SEX, 'TIL DEATH DO YOU PART?

INTRODUCTION

You'll never believe what I have found to be one of the top reasons women are frustrated with their husbands, and it's not the old *putting down the toilet seat* argument.

It's that husbands have stopped taking the initiative to show their wives how much they love them. Think about it: women are absolutely exhausted from working all day plus taking care of the kids and the home. They are doing two jobs! And the husbands have stopped romancing their wives like they did when they were dating. It's no wonder that they have little interest in sex.

But I have a secret. You know what turns a woman on? It's when her husband calls her Friday afternoon and tells her to be ready at 6 pm for dinner and a movie. And when she asks "but what about the kids?" he confidently replies "I have that taken care of!" This is what every woman wants, and the man that does this consistently gets what he wants in return; a loving and appreciative wife!

In *The Man's Secret to a Happy and Sexy Marriage in Less Than 10 Minutes a Day*, I share with you what I have learned after a twenty-four year marriage, a lousy divorce, years of dating and now being in a wonderfully loving relationship. When I was married, it was taboo to talk to other guys about marriage problems. Heaven forbid you told your friends that your marriage was on the rocks and your sex life too.

When I look back on my marriage I realize not only the good things that I did, but I also recognize the things that I neglected to do that could have possibly saved my marriage. You see, I loved my wife when we walked down the aisle, but over time we grew apart. There were a number of factors that put a strain on the relationship, including health and work issues. These things, particularly in the early years of a marriage, can have quite an impact on the love, friendship and intimacy in a relationship. And sometimes no matter what you do, it is difficult to dig yourself out of that hole.

For me, I stuck around for the children as I

wanted to take an active role in their lives. During their formative years, the kids were such a distraction that the relationship was on the back burner. But over time, as the kids matured and required less attention, I realized that the way my wife and I interacted negatively impacted my self-confidence and I felt like sex was used as leverage against me. Believe me when I tell you, and you may be able to relate, that it is very easy to get sucked into an unhappy marriage and not realize it for a long time. Instead of being selfless to each other like when you were newly married, the dynamics of the relationship change and you just don't notice what has happened. I actually came to accept my situation as normal, thinking this is just what happens after you get married. Then one day you have a "wake-up call" where you realize you are not happy and things need to be fixed NOW!

The Man's Secret to a Happy and Sexy Marriage will show you a new way of communicating with your wife so that you can hopefully skip months or years of marriage counseling and even forgo divorce. All you really need to do is make simple changes to how you interact with your wife *in less than 10 minutes a day* to reawaken the feelings of security and love that you have for each other.

I ran into an industry friend while writing this book who happened to share with me the challenges of his marriage. He said that he truly loves his wife and wants to be sure that she always knows how much he loves her. When I told him about my forthcoming book and the list of "101 Ways to a Sexy Marriage", he asked if I could share a copy with him. Lo and behold, he tried just one thing on the list and this is the email I received in return:

"I did number 7 this weekend! Great stuff. Thank you for the inspiration!"

After incorporating just a few of the many ideas and concepts, your wife will be shocked! When that happens, watch to see how she speaks to you more lovingly and also becomes more intimate in return! Don't be surprised when she brags to her girlfriends about her wonderful, sexy *new* husband. This could cause quite a problem for *their* husbands!

I have by design written this book in hopes that you will read each chapter carefully as the material is rich in content with lots of concepts, perspectives and ideas to consider. I am also hoping that you find *The Man's Secret* so beneficial that you refer to it often. Nothing would make me happier than meeting you at a book signing where the cover of your book is all crinkled, numerous pages are dog-eared, notes are written throughout—and you with a big smile on your face!

Steve Schloss

THE BEST
KEPT SECRET

The 1% Rule That Saves Marriages

THE SCHLOSS LEAD IN

1. *What is the 1% Rule?*
2. *How can you apply the 1% rule to your marriage?*
3. *Go Rock her world!*

HOW WAS THE
1% RULE CREATED?

> "In a good relationship, every day is Valentine's Day"

I was in a twenty-four year marriage. It is not what I would call a successful marriage. In fact, it was a pretty terrible marriage for the last five years. There was no communication, a lot of fighting and definitely no intimacy. It seemed to me that intimacy was used as leverage to influence my behavior.

I wanted to be with my children every day while they were young, so I stayed in the marriage. My goal was to survive every day with the least amount of conflict possible. But there came a day when my son, the younger of two children, entered high school. That is when I decided that enough was enough. It was time to stop the madness.

I always try to learn from my experiences, be them positive or negative. Could there be something beneficial to gain from my marriage? My married years felt very belittling for me. I made most of the money, yet I never felt like I wore the proverbial pants in the household. My opinions and feelings never seemed to be acknowledged as anything of value. And when I tried to be romantic, my gestures were usually rejected.

After many years of feeling like I was imperfect and inadequate, I actually started to believe that there was something wrong with me. However, I had a wakeup call—and that wakeup call was meeting other women. Women who actually found me to be funny, handsome, intelligent and desirable. I had to pinch myself!

When I married my wife, I truly loved her and planned on spending the rest of my life in blissful matrimony. But as the marriage evolved, it seemed that our communication became more strained. In addition, my romantic advances were received less positively and typically failed to improve our feelings of love for each other. Perhaps the way I communicated led her to believe that there was a motive behind my treating her nicely. Intimacy was a struggle and seemed to be a bone of contention even if I gave her what she wanted, like an evening on the town. So at some point, I just gave up trying. It felt to me that the relationship was too one-sided.

Does any of this sound remotely familiar to you in your marriage?

I even recall when I would bring home flowers as a gesture of love that they would always end up in the garbage can. My wife, I believe, thought I was bringing her flowers for the sole purpose of wanting sex. But that was not the intention. I really loved her and wanted to make her feel special and adored.

At one point we went to marriage counseling to try and remedy the situation. We only met with the therapist four or five times. At the end of the last session he politely asked my wife to leave the room, wanting to speak with me privately. After she left the room, he bluntly said to me "this marriage cannot be saved". To which I replied "thank you, you've saved me a lot of time and money". The next day I called a lawyer.

In my twenty-second year of marriage, my wife and I separated once and for all. I moved into a two-bedroom apartment and started dating again. It was not easy as I had a lot of healing and confidence to regain within myself. But being a student of human nature, I noticed that even the smallest acts of attention and romance were greatly appreciated by other women. A lot of the women I dated were separated or newly divorced, so they were fresh out of emotionally draining relationships themselves. They had gone years without any acknowledgment or appreciation from their husbands.

In the first three years after separation, I dated a lot of women and am now in a wonderful relationship. During this time, I have talked to hundreds of people—both men and women—about their marriages and relationships. I talked to people I met on airplanes, in coffee shops, at business lunches and anywhere I could strike up a conversation about love and marriage. People felt pretty open to talk to me as I typically start talking about my own experiences first. I did not conduct scientific research, but here are some generalizations that I recognized from my own observations:

- When couples get married, they oftentimes get complacent and stop doing a lot of the things that bonded them in the first place.

- Women need to be listened to, romanced and adored by their men.

- Men need to feel appreciated by their wives.

- A healthy relationship is the responsibility of the man. Men need to be the initiators when it comes to communication and romance.

- Women need to feel connected to have sex.

- Men need to have sex to feel connected.

- A lot of marriages get in a rut, but there is a possibility for couples to dig out of that hole by changing or reactivating a few basic behaviors.

With the divorce rate around 50%, it is my

belief that most married couples are just going through the motions of pretending to be happy. How often do you see couples in public sitting together yet not conversing or smiling with each other? How often have you seen couples at parties not talking to their significant other the entire evening? Thankfully there are one or two couples that actually spend some time together at social events, talking to and touching each other endearingly.

So here I was, now a single man again, spending a lot of time thinking about and fascinated by interpersonal relationships. Then one day I read an interesting statistic. It said that the average married couple spends only 7 1/2 minutes per day talking to each other. The typical couple finds very little time to actually talk to each other and stay bonded with all the craziness of being married, raising children, walking the dog, cleaning the house and running to dance classes and soccer practices. The time spent together actually grows shorter as the years pass (and the relationship worsens). Yet when they first meet, the happy couple spent hours upon hours talking to each other and building a relationship. This is what I term the "Communication Breakdown".

Then I had a light bulb go off in my head. If the average couple spends only around seven minutes per day talking, and a lot of that is actually non-relationship building conversation, could their relationship be improved—even reinvigorated—with just a slight modification in behavior?

This was my epiphany, as well as the catalyst for the title and purpose of this book—the birth of what I call "The 1% Rule That Saves Marriages".

If you only read the first chapter of this book and apply this simple solution, your relationship has the opportunity to improve immensely—even immediately! Of course, there are a lot of other valuable perspectives and ideas to improve your marriage throughout the book. But if this is all you read, then I venture to say that you will find this a worthy investment of your time.

THE 1% RULE DEFINED

The 1% Rule is so easy; I am almost embarrassed to share it. The 1% Rule has been transformational, not only in my relationships but also in other areas of my life.

There are 24 hours in any given day. Eight hours are typically used for sleep, and the remaining 16 hours are for when we are awake *during* the day.

During those 16 waking hours, there are 960 minutes available to work, eat, do leisure activities and spend time with friends and family.

One percent of those 16 waking hours is only 9 minutes and 36 seconds.

If you were to pay undivided attention to your wife for *just* 9 1/2 minutes per day, how much would your wife appreciate that? Remember, a woman needs attention and communication to feel connected to her man. I bet you could greatly improve your relationship, and probably also your sex life, by employing what I share with you in this chapter.

Do you recall how much attention you focused on your wife when you initially met her and before you got married? How about the level of intimacy you shared with her too? That is what we are shooting for here!

And the 9 1/2 minutes doesn't have to be consumed all at once. In fact, the more you cut it up into smaller increments, the more she will appreciate you and your efforts. From my experience, women need to hear that you care about them at least five times a day to feel connected and loved.

How can the 9 1/2 minutes be best utilized to maximize effectiveness in improving your marriage?

Below is a list of nine ways you can communicate with your wife during the day so that she knows how much you adore her and that you can't wait to spend more time with her. With the advances of digital technology (e.g. texting and email), we now have many ways to stay connected. Just be sure that the things you say and do are true to your heart and totally sincere. Your wife will be able to tell if are "faking it", which will defeat the whole purpose. In addition to the actions, I have allocated the amount of time it takes to do each activity.

9 WAYS TO APPLY THE 1% RULE USING JUST 4 ½ MINUTES!

1. When you wake up in the morning, tell your wife how happy you are to be married to her and how much you love her: 15 seconds.

2. Text her during the day that you can't wait to hug her when you get home: 15 seconds.

3. If you made love to your wife the night before, leave a note on the windshield of her car or on top of her purse telling her how sexy she is and how much you love her: 30 seconds.

4. Take a photo on your cell phone of you posing like you are giving your wife a big kiss. Say in the text box "I Love You", and then send it to her: 30 seconds.

5. Call her during the day to see how her day is going, and tell her that you can't wait to get home to hear more about it: one minute.

6. Post a romantic poem or quote on your wife's Facebook © page: 30 seconds.

7. Give her a big hug when you first see each other after work. Look her in the eyes and tell her how much you love her: 30 seconds.

8. Rub your wife's shoulders for 45 seconds before you sit down for dinner.

9. When you are done and she stops moaning, put your mouth next to her ear and whisper "I love you so much": 15 seconds.

So far this is just 270 seconds, or 4 1/2 minutes of your 9 1/2 minute allotment. Look at all the wonderful things you have done to make your wife feel adored and cared for, yet you still have over half of your 9 1/2 minutes left. In fact, you still have over five minutes left to talk about her day or to cuddle, laugh and remind her how much you love her when you are in bed together.

You see, it is not difficult to do the things that will make your wife happy. And the best thing is it doesn't even cost any money to give your wife the most valuable thing in her life: *your attention and love.*

Buying your wife flowers, chocolates and a nice juicy steak dinner for Valentine's Day is nice. However, treating her special every day is more appreciated and valued by most women. It is also the basis of a healthy, loving relationship. When I visit my girlfriend's home, where she is still raising teenage children, I will often spend a few minutes after walking in the door to put dishes in the dishwasher or pick up in general. You can't believe how much appreciation I get for making her hectic life a little bit easier. She has even said that bringing her flowers on occasion is really nice, but helping her like I just explained makes her know how much I truly love her.

I have a friend who told me that she and her husband have sex approximately every other day, and she has noticed that her husband always cleans the dishes in the kitchen sink on the days when he wants to be intimate. Guess it's not just me who uses a clean kitchen as a romantic precursor! The interesting thing is that if he decides that he wants sex on one of the "off" days, he does the dishes that day too. Otherwise he lets the dishes go. How funny is that!

When we are busy at work, it is difficult prioritizing your wife into your busy day. However, there is nothing more important in your life than your loved one's relationship. Jobs, friends and work colleagues may come and go, but your wife is here for you day in and day out—through thick and thin. She should be your number one priority! If your marriage is good, you will feel a lot more confident and productive in everything else you do.

HE MADE HER
MELT LIKE BUTTER

I was talking to my friend Phil one day, and he told me that his wife Ellen had been complaining about their relationship. She regularly mentions that he doesn't pay her the same type or amount of attention as he did earlier in their relationship. Phil said that he is so busy every week, literally racing against the clock, trying to keep up with work and projects around the house, that he really doesn't have time to interact with his wife very much. Then, when they go to bed at night, his sexual advances are rejected on a regular basis. What a shocker! You just can't expect your wife to want to have sex if you haven't made her feel loved prior to bedtime.

So I shared with Phil my idea of the 1% Rule, and he said that he would give it a shot.

After a few weeks, Phil ccstatically called me about how his relationship had improved with Ellen. He said that at first his wife thought what he was doing was kind of weird or perhaps out of character. But he persisted and she melted like butter in his hands when she saw that he was sincere, truly loved her and wanted to have a great marriage.

I asked him to share some of the things he did that really turned things around.

Phil said that leaving notes, sending text messages during the day and even bringing home flowers were all warmly received by his wife. However, the one thing that his wife loves the most is performed when they go out together. When they go to the car, first he opens the door for her. After Ellen sits down, Phil grabs the seat belt, reaches across her and buckles her in. He then looks her in the eyes, gives her a big hug and kiss, and states that he loves her. He then struts to the other side of the car and gets behind the steering wheel. When he looks over at the passenger seat, his wife has the biggest smile on her face. And Phil feels like such a man.

PUTTING THE 1% RULE TO PRACTICE

I started to put the 1% Rule to the test during my three years of dating. But it was not until I met my girlfriend that I saw how totally effective it could be in keeping a relationship fresh, connected and passionate on a day-to-day basis.

It is so easy in daily life to get wrapped up in all the monotony of work, activities and family. Yet taking just a few minutes here and there throughout the day to reconnect with your partner makes a world of difference. The key is to be totally sincere that you want to listen to and adore her.

For me, here are a few examples of my typical day with my girlfriend:

- I will kiss my girlfriend goodbye in the morning and tell her how beautiful she is! In response, she will get a big smile on her face and tell me that she loves me back.

- I will text her during the day that I miss her, and she will text me back that she can't wait to hug me when we see each other.

- I will call or text her a few times during the day to see how she is doing. If I am super busy, I will let her know that I only have a minute or two to talk but wanted to hear her voice, see how she was doing and let her know that I miss her. She will appreciate that I took the time to think about her. At the end of the conversation or texting I will tell her I love her, and she will tell me she loves me back.

- When eating a meal, I make a point of sitting next to her so that I can touch her arms and legs. It also allows me to lean over and whisper sweet things into her ear.

After a day of incorporating the 1% Rule, how do you think my girlfriend responds to me when we get into bed at night? We can't wait to touch each other's naked bodies and snuggle. Even if we don't have sex, our hugs and kisses are extremely passionate. Also, we always say that we love each other before we fall asleep in each other's arms.

When we do have disagreements, as all couples do, I tell her how important it is that we talk about it. In fact, I am pretty darn adamant that we always communicate honestly and sincerely, especially during difficult times. When I was married, I didn't communicate but rather felt like I was lectured by my wife. Now, however, I feel like I am the man in my relationship and insist that we talk things out before we go to bed. Then we kiss, hug and are reminded how much we care for each other. It is such a beautiful thing that I never had in my marriage or other relationships.

The best way to start using the 1% Rule is to incorporate it into your daily life. Like any new learned behavior, practice makes perfect. If you are positively reinforced, it will become a regular part of your daily routine.

I suggest that you start by making a list of just five to ten things that you can do for your wife during the day that will remind her how much you love her. These will be things that will reinforce your relationship and make her want to please you with reciprocal appreciation and love. They should be things that will flow from your relationship and sound natural. You may want to start conservatively with things that are appropriate for where you are in the relationship. For example, you may only feel comfortable initially letting her know how beautiful she is, how much you love her and how much you can't wait to hug her when you get home. But as your relationship improves and she becomes more receptive to the *new you*, you may want to try spicing it up a bit with playful, sexually suggestive teasing in order to see how she responds. Wouldn't it be great to get to the point where you can send her the text message, "Can't wait to kiss you all over tonight, starting with your feet and moving all the way up to your lips", and then she responds with a smiley face?

What I did when I started practicing the 1% Rule was to create a mental or written list of a few things that I wanted to do that day for the woman in my life. I wanted there to be some variety, so I would brainstorm three to five different things to do that day and when to do them. I would even set the alarm on my wrist watch to remind me to do something such as a text, call or email. It is so easy to get wrapped up at work that I knew I needed reminders. I suggest that you come up with a method that works for you in order to remind yourself. Try setting some reminders in your work email system so that an alarm goes off (e.g. once at 10am and another at 3pm).

It really helps to come up with a method where you can remind yourself to implement the rules for the day. Even if your wife happens to come across your reminders, just tell her that you love her so much that you want her to know it in her heart. The key is being totally sincere in your communication so that she knows it is not contrived; it is important to show that you really love her and want to have a wonderful marriage.

After you do this for a while, it will become habitual, and you won't have to remind yourself quite so often.

MY BOYFRIEND
GETS IT NOW!

I shared the concept of the 1% Rule with a co-worker named Selena a few years ago, and she thought it was a great idea. We work in different departments and on different floors, so we actually only run into each other every month or so. When I last saw her, she inquired as to the progress I was making with the book. I told her that I had the first chapter written in rough form and what it was about. She responded, "Could I have a copy to share with my boyfriend Ramon? He has not been that attentive to me the past few months as he is busy getting his new business off the ground. I know that he really loves me, and maybe this will resonate about what I need in our relationship." So, of course, I shared the draft of the 1% Rule.

About a month went by and I received a call from Selena. She said that the chapter was a "wake up call" for her boyfriend, and Ramon actually started to pay more attention to her emotional needs in the relationship. She said that he started to do really cute things throughout the day that made her feel special and loved. Selena also mentioned, with a wink, that their sex life improved too.

When I asked Selena if it bothered her that her boyfriend's actions were a result of reading the chapter, she said that she didn't care at all. She knew that Ramon needed a kick in the pants, and this was the perfect thing. She was just so happy that his new behavior improved their relationship, and they even joke from time to time about how he is using the 1% Rule to romance her.

PIZZA AND FIREWORKS

I also notice how effective the 1% Rule can be in social situations. For example, my girlfriend and I recently had a New Year's Eve party. We had to pick up some food a few hours before the party started because restaurants were closing early. When our guests started to arrive, I took the initiative to turn on the oven and warm the pizza and wings. As people were starting to get hungry, I already had the food ready to go.

My actions took all of three minutes out of the entire five hours we had company. Three minutes ironically equates to my spending just 1% of the entire evening taking care of this minor, yet highly important task. When I brought the hot food out of the kitchen, the female guests noticed what I did and asked my girlfriend where she found me. They were so surprised to see a man do this, particularly without a woman asking him to do it first. And as for my girlfriend, she gave me a big smile and thanked me. Think we started our New Year's with some fireworks?

GO ROCK
HER WORLD!

Try the 1% Rule for a week, and see how your wife is a changed woman. If she ever asks why you are acting like this, tell her that you just want her to know how much you love and appreciate her being in your life.

By implementing the 1% Rule, your wife will be so happy and want to tell her friends how romantic you have become toward her. Your communication will improve, and she will become more affectionate and receptive to your advances for intimacy. Even your children and friends will notice a change in how you both interact with each other. Isn't it worth just 9 1/2 minutes a day to have better communication, fewer fights and more sex?

Now that you've had some time to think about

it and read a few stories, take a few minutes right now to write down 15 to 20 things that you can do to romance your wife during the day. Women love anticipation, so turn it into a game. Keep thinking of new things you can do to surprise her and demonstrate your love. Start with messages that are not very sexually suggestive but instead are endearing, like how you miss and love her or want to hug and kiss her. Then after a while, you can make your communication more sexually suggestive if you think she will be receptive to that. Remember, this is all about romancing your wife. You will be so glad that you did!

PLEASE TAKE OFF YOUR SHOES, LEAVE YOUR
PAYCHECK ON THE TABLE AND HANG UP
YOUR BALLS!

THE PENDULUM
OF POWER
WITHIN MARRIAGE

THE SCHLOSS LEAD IN

1. *The Pendulum of Power Defined*
2. *The 3 Stages of Power in Relationships*
3. *Understand Your Position, and Stop the Insanity*

"The person who is more emotionally attached will have less power in the relationship"

After reading about the 1% Rule, do you feel that these ideas will benefit your relationship and intimacy? Or do you believe that there are other considerations in your marriage that may prohibit the 1% Rule from being a positive influence on your marriage? Are there past issues within your marriage that prevent your wife from sharing intimacy with you even though you now show her how much you love her? It is important to understand how you possibly got into the current circumstance of your marriage.

For many couples, the roles in the marriage change over time. Whereas the man wore the proverbial pants before the wedding, the woman may wear them now. I've talked to a lot of women about their relationships and have heard some common complaints. Women would like their husbands to take on shares of responsibility (e.g. raising the children and taking care of the house), as well as take some control of their social lives including romance. These factors are what women typically perceive as someone being a *Real Man*.

I recall having lunch with a client many years ago in Ohio. He told me that he was married with three young children. We were talking about marriage and relationships, and I vividly recall him telling me that he was not big on watching sports or drinking beers with the guys: activities most men would associate with being macho. Yet, he felt that he was an extremely masculine man because he took responsibility for loving his wife and raising a family. Ain't that the truth!

When the husband does not support the woman and romance her, it is no surprise the wife has little interest in intimacy with her husband. Women seek men who provide comfort and security in their lives. If they don't get it, it is difficult for them to show love in return.

So how does the man get back his stature in the relationship so that his wife finds him attractive and desirable?

I have surveyed many women, and they realize that they have a lot of power in the marriage. Most husbands are dependent on their wives for domestic related things like food, clean clothes and an organized home. Women also have control over their husband's sexual satisfaction.

I went to have my hair cut recently (what little hair I have left!) and got to talking to my stylist, Annette, about the book I was writing. I shared with her the concept of The 1% Rule and my thoughts on power within relationships. We have a very open relationship, so I felt comfortable asking her where she thinks the power lies within a marriage. Without hesitation, Annette replied quite seriously that she believes women have a lot of power in relationships. I asked her why, and she said "Because women have control over sex."

The truth is a woman really wants her husband to be the man of the household. She wants to be romanced and treated special. She doesn't want so much of the burden of the marriage to fall on her. She wants to be cared for, romanced and loved both in and out of the bedroom.

The key is finding a balance between the emotional and the physical.

THE PENDULUM
OF POWER

In relationships, it is not unusual for one person to have more power or leverage over the other person. Leverage can swing back and forth between husband and wife throughout the marriage. A little imbalance here or there is normal. It is when the proverbial balance in the relationship is swinging more to one side that the marriage is really not a marriage at all. Instead of being an equal partnership, it feels more like one person being a prisoner at the mercy of a heartless captor.

A good friend of mine, Bob, fell in love with his bride-to-be, Sue, after he graduated from college. Bob was introduced to Sue by a mutual friend. It was Bob's first serious relationship, and he had never experienced such amazing passion before in his life. Sue really liked Bob a lot, so she tried to make him happy by doing a lot of the things that he liked to do. She also pampered him with lots of attention and gave him sex like he had never experienced before in his life. As a result, Bob had amazing confidence in himself; you could envision him pounding his chest like the king of the jungle. Bob certainly had the balance leaning in his direction, as Sue was using all of her femininity to make Bob feel as loving toward her as possible.

Things were going along marvelously until one day, after two years of dating, Sue gave Bob an ultimatum. She wanted to get married, and she told Bob that either he proposes or she would move on and look for someone else. Bob was in charge of making the decision to either advance the relationship or end it. Bob had the power even more severely tipped in his favor, as Sue wanted something really badly from Bob: a proposal.

Bob, being unsure of his emotions and also fearful of ever finding another woman in his life, took the bait and proposed to her. From that moment on their connection was still good, but the dynamics of the relationship started to change as did the frequency of sex. Bob, being accustomed to a great sex life, was confused as to why his now future bride was less interested in intimacy with him—particularly giving oral sex. At this point, the balance not only evened out but started to swing in the favor of Sue. You see, Bob was starting to feel rejected and at the mercy of Sue for his sexual satisfaction. What before came as a result of strength was now disappearing as a sign of weakness in the relationship.

As the wedding day got closer, Bob noticed that the love in the relationship grew more strained and the frequency of sex came even less often. He felt that Sue was getting more difficult to please. They were so busy with the wedding plans that the romance in the relationship had taken a back seat. Plus, the decrease in sexual satisfaction affected Bob's emotions toward Sue. He truly felt rejected now. However, he was afraid to address it with Sue, as the big day was just around the corner. Bob was starting to wonder if he was making a mistake marrying this woman, but he continued to rationalize that Sue was temporarily distracted due all the wedding arrangements. He hoped and prayed once the wedding was over that things would return to normal. But what would the *new* normal be? His insecurity allowed Sue to maintain and grow her power over him.

Instead of remaining proactive in the relationship, Bob started to be a *yes man* by positively reacting to whatever Sue wanted. He had not taken the lead in the relationship in quite some time now. His strategy, if there was one, was to constantly ask Sue what she wanted. His goal was to do whatever he could to try and please her. He figured that if she was emotionally happy, she would feel more loving towards him and also be more open to having sex with her fiancée. But that didn't seem to work very well!

When the wedding day came, the newlyweds left on a honeymoon to Europe. Sadly, there wasn't much playfulness between them and sex on the honeymoon was almost non-existent. Bob was really dumbfounded, as he wondered how this could have happened on his honeymoon. Honeymoons were supposed to be the most fun and romantic time in a marriage. Whatever happened to the loving woman that he dated? Even though he still had feelings of love for Sue, he didn't know how much longer he could endure a cold relationship and sexual rejection.

At this point, it became clear that Bob

relinquished all sense of power to Sue. She got her marriage, she controlled Bob's emotional and physical pleasure and she had him wrapped around her little finger. If she said jump, he would literally hit his head on the ceiling if he knew it would result in a more fun and intimate marriage. Yet, he was locked into a marital situation where he was morally prohibited from seeking any form of emotional or physical pleasure elsewhere. What was he to do? How did he get himself in this mess?

It is interesting to note that Bob is not alone. Many married men have shared with me a similar experience of not having romance on their honeymoon. They also hinted that intimacy has been a challenge for most of their married life. One friend even joked quite sarcastically that his favorite form of foreplay with his wife is "four weeks of begging and pleading."

You might ask, why would Sue stop being intimate with Bob? Were there ulterior motives to the marriage? Was she just not as sexual of a woman as Bob thought? Was Bob not addressing some of the needs that Sue needed from her husband? Was Sue now focused on fulfilling other things in her life after securing a husband?

Bob was miserable and desperately needed an answer! He truly felt that he was a good man and tried to do everything he could to make his wife happy. However, he still felt like he was being treated like a dog: sitting by the master's feet and waiting for scraps to be dropped on the floor. It was really sad!

When we meet someone and get married, we never totally understand the person's motivations and personality, nor do we fully understand our own. You see, emotions have a funny way of blurring reality. When we get into an emotional relationship, we lose a certain amount of objectivity that often leads us into making decisions without clarity. This is what makes selecting a life partner so difficult. It's unfortunate we aren't taught this in school!

NANCY AND BARRY

Another couple, Nancy and Barry, were married for a number of years. Their marriage started out really good, but over time their relationship evolved to being almost like roommates. Barry and Nancy had two children ages 7 and 10. They were so busy managing family and work that they didn't spend a lot of time focusing on each other. Nancy also had a long commute to and from work, leaving her tired and seemingly without much energy for her husband. Yet Barry, who worked from home, had interest in a fun and intimate marriage. This started to cause quite a bit of tension between the couple. Barry, loving his wife yet not knowing what to do, started to do everything he could to try and keep Nancy happy. She obviously had the power in this relationship, as Nancy was controlling the type of marriage that Barry wanted.

To try and reduce Nancy's stress, Barry washed the dishes after dinner, vacuumed on the weekends, prepared most meals and even did the laundry. However, their intimacy did not improve. Nancy still refused to have sex with Barry. Was there something besides Nancy being tired that resulted in her lack of intimacy towards Barry? Even when Barry took Nancy out for that rare evening on the town, Nancy refused to be playful! As push came to shove, she even went as far as telling Barry that his sex drive was abnormally strong and that there was something wrong with him. Barry allowed himself to have no power in this marriage!

Over time, Barry actually started to believe that there *was* something wrong with him. Maybe he did have an unusually strong sex drive and sex after marriage was supposed to be infrequent. He heard other men joke about having to kowtow to their wives—was this the new normal after marriage? Was there possibly something else causing this situation that Barry couldn't figure out? Was this comparable to a person having numerous disease symptoms, yet being unable to diagnose the cause?

Then the day came where Barry could take it no longer and he had to talk to someone about it. So he called a friend of his who is a lawyer and shared his story. The lawyer suggested that Barry and Nancy see a marriage counselor. At first Nancy refused. But Barry persisted and told his wife that if she didn't go that he would be filing for divorce. When he said these words to her and saw her reaction, this was the first time in years Barry felt like he regained some power.

The good news is counseling revealed that Nancy had been abused as a child and something had triggered these emotions, resulting in her change of behavior toward Barry. Over time, they were able to resolve their problems, regain a loving partnership and rebalance the power in the marriage. Beautiful!

WHO HAS
THE POWER?

In relationships, as in these stories, there is always one person who has more power or influence over the other person. I define power as one person having something that the other person wants and thus being able to manipulate the other person's behavior. For example, it could be one person using the power of money to get the other person to do things. Another example would be your manager at work having power over you because you need a job to pay the bills and support the family.

In a family, the parents have leverage over their children, because the parents have final say as to what things the children can have and do. Remember when you were a kid how you had to beg your parents when you wanted to go to a concert or buy something? In exchange, your parents asked you to promise to keep a cleaner bedroom or walk the dog more often—like that ever happened!

When men and women are dating and even married, one person typically has more power over the other because there is an unequal balance of emotional commitment in the relationship. The attachment can be physical or emotional (e.g. sex and love) or materialistic (e.g. money). This results in one person working harder in the relationship to try and satisfy his/her needs. If a man makes most of the money and the woman is very materialistic, the woman will dote on her man to get the materialistic things that make her happy. If a woman doesn't care about sex as much as her man, the man will dote on his woman to try and get his needs satisfied. The person who wants something from the other will suck up to the other person. Sucking up, however, is demeaning and does not result in gaining respect from the other person.

Do you think a woman will want to make love to a man she doesn't respect?

Understanding the dynamics of power in a relationship is essential to regaining mutual respect and gaining some insight into your particular marital situation.

DEFINING THE 3 STAGES
TO THE POWER EQUATION

There are 3 stages to the *Power Equation*. In each stage, one person has more influence over the other person.

STAGE 1

This is when a man and woman first meet. Let's say that Tom sees Margie at a party. They are on opposite sides of the room while holding drinks and talking to other people. Tom keeps looking at Margie to appreciate her smile, beautiful figure and long blonde hair. He decides that he wants to meet her and saunters across the room to introduce himself.

You would think that Tom has the power in this situation, as he has taken the initiative to approach Margie. In reality, Margie has the power to accept or reject Tom's advance. Tom wants to get to know Margie, so Margie has control over what Tom wants. Thus, Margie has the power. If she accepts Tom, she has the power to influence his behavior (e.g. calling her, taking her on dates, etc.).

If Margie continues to find Tom attractive and interesting after a few dates, she will start to get more intimate with Tom. She will accept his touching, kissing and eventually sex. This is when the power starts to even out. There is now mutual interest.

STAGE 2

As Margie and Tom continue to date and Margie gets feelings for a more serious relationship with Tom, she relinquishes a large part of her power to him. You see, Margie now wants Tom to commit to her as a boyfriend and potential future husband. Tom has what Margie wants.

Margie still has some power in the relationship. She is still quite effective in getting Tom to wine and dine her at fancy restaurants, bring her flowers and get him to do other romantic things that are part of the *mating dance.*

While the relationship further evolves and Margie gets even more interested in Tom as a potential mate, Tom's power escalates because he now has something that she really desires. As a result, Margie uses all of her resources (e.g. sexuality) to try to get Tom to commit. Do you remember how awesome sex was during this time in your courtship?

Tom's power is now in full throttle. He is pumped up and feels like the king of the jungle. He has all the power in the relationship, as Margie wants Tom to commit to her. As a result, Tom is getting the best sex of his life.

STAGE 3

Once Tom starts to take the relationship more seriously and commits to Margie, the power starts to swing back to her. Should they get married, then the power is fully back in Margie's court. If Tom is a sexual male, Margie now has total control over Tom's sexual satisfaction. If Tom and Margie get married, Tom is now legally beholden to Margie for his sexual gratification. The legal aspect of marriage makes the power Margie has over Tom even stronger.

Men rarely understand this equation until they are married, and then it is too late. The net result is men often become the weaker sex in their marriage, turning into "yes men". They stop being the confident men that their wives were attracted to in the first place. Instead, they will do whatever their wives ask with the hopes and prayers of getting their sexual desires fulfilled. I have an acquaintance that went to extremes in order to improve his love life. He and his wife lived in an older house where the husband was comfortable, but his wife wanted to live in a more modern, larger environment. Their sex life was almost non-existent, so he was desperate for a solution. One day she told her husband that she would feel more loving toward him if they moved into a new, larger home. She got her new home. Their intimacy didn't improve!

I was talking to a client of mine, Mike, and he said that he has never had a problem with sex in his marriage. He is one of the few men I have ever met who understood the power equation before he got married! Mike told me that he set a mandate with his fiancée before they walked down the aisle. He told her, "If you get headaches, I get girlfriends." It was that simple. Mike set a precedent that sex was not going to be a bargaining chip in his marriage.

I must add that Mike shared he is a very loving husband (and father now, too) and works very hard to give his wife the things that she needs in marriage. Obviously if he did not treat her well, she probably would not have sex with him.

So how does the man get back his manhood? How does he take back the power that he may have unconsciously relinquished to the woman?

It is so easy for a man to be preoccupied with work and other things in life that he doesn't objectively see himself in the marriage. He leaves the house in the morning, works hard all day long and typically doesn't talk to his wife during business hours unless there is an emergency. When he gets home he just wants to have dinner, relax and make love to his wife before they go to bed. If he isn't getting the sex he wants, he takes the path of least resistance. The man tries to avoid any confrontation and gives in to most of his wife's wishes thinking that this will make her want to have sex with him. He is not consciously aware of this behavior. As his need for sex begins to possess his mind, the man kicks into what I call "sex survival mode". He does whatever he thinks it will take to have his desire for sex fulfilled.

In the next chapter, we will review what your wife needs from you in the marriage so that she will want to please you in return. Remember what I said earlier: the man has the responsibility to manage the relationship, and women usually want the man to take the lead. It is when men stop being proactive that the walls of intimacy crumble.

STOP THE INSANITY!

To improve your marriage you will need to break old habits. Have you heard the definition of insanity? Insanity is doing the same thing over and over again and expecting the results to be different than the time before. If you continue to beg, plead or grope for sex and things don't change, you will need to revise your strategy.

I have a friend, Mark, who has been married for over 10 years. He makes a good living and does whatever his wife asks him to do around the house. Mark shared with me, however, that when he goes to sleep at night he is extremely sexually frustrated. His wife just doesn't want to make love to him. He doesn't know what to do, so he reverts to pawing at her (e.g. grabbing at her breasts and rubbing up against her) thinking that maybe this will turn her on. But, this perpetual behavior does not result in a different outcome. Mark has to figure out why this is happening and come up with a new strategy. Even if Mark's wife does relinquish and have sex with him on occasion, it ends up being mercy sex aimed to shut him up and leave her alone for a while.

So who has the power in your marriage? What do you need to do in order to regain those feelings of intimacy like when you met? How can you get your wife to lust over you and view you once again like her roman warrior? What can you do to get her to yearn for your naked body and want to please you?

THE A-LIST
THAT LEADS TO A
SEXY MARRIAGE

THE SCHLOSS LEAD IN

1. *How is your relationship with your wife?*
2. *Do you understand what your wife needs from you in the marriage?*
3. *Do you have a plan to give your wife what she needs?*

> "The glass is only half full when you don't mix the emotions with the action"

We now realize that we have to make more of a time investment in the marriage by applying principles from the 1% Rule, as well as have a better understanding of any imbalance of power. Both factors may have contributed to your current state of affairs. It is now time to address the needs of the relationship. What exactly do women need from their husbands to have a successful marriage? How can you best satisfy each other's needs? What can you do to ensure long-term happiness? When you understand these needs, you can then apply them to your use of the 1% Rule and hence maximize the love, intimacy and fun in your marriage.

BE A SUPER HERO, AND SAVE YOUR MARRIAGE

When I think of power, I often think of the super heroes I grew up with (e.g. Superman or Batman). My family always had dinner together when my father got home from work. But on the nights that Batman was on TV, I was allowed to eat dinner sitting in front of the TV in the family room. The super hero's role was not to just be powerful and save the day but also to teach a lesson in understanding how to use power properly. Their enemies had power too, but they were trying to use it to the detriment of society. The super heroes had a moral obligation to use their power to benefit mankind.

When your wife starts to really enjoy the

attention and love you share with her, you start to take back some of the power in your marriage. She now has something that she enjoys receiving from you that satisfies her needs for a loving relationship. It is your duty to use your power responsibly. Your wife will hopefully realize that she cannot use her sexuality to manipulate your behavior in getting what she needs from the marriage. She will also understand that you want to have a fun, loving and intimate relationship. However, love is a two-way street. Both people need to be selfless and think about what the other person needs in order to live a happy life. If each person provides those things, then a truly loving partnership can exist. But, this is no easy task. Life is not static, and there is no game plan to follow to ensure success. If only it were as simple as connecting the dots!

STICKING TO THE BASICS IS KEY

If you were to gauge or rate the success of your marriage on a scale of one to ten with ten being the best, how would rate it?

Now that you have a number in mind, let's look at some basic concepts to make it better.

In the game of football, the Super Bowl champion has to score more touchdowns, week in and week out, to reach the pinnacle of their sport. To score touchdowns, the team definitely needs to know how to execute the basics of the sport: blocking, tackling, running, passing and kicking. But the team that is most successful doesn't just execute their offense and defense the same way every play. The team needs to study how best to apply the basics under different circumstances.

For example, every team knows how to block. Your team could have the biggest, strongest offensive linemen in the league. But if they block in the wrong direction, the running back may get tackled behind the line of scrimmage.

This same philosophy also applies to your job. You need to learn the basics of your job and then understand how to use those skills in different situations. Why do you think managers are usually older than everyone else at work? Because they have years of experience under their belts to make the best decisions and help their company be successful. Much of this same effort that goes into a successful sports team and work environment applies to success in marriage. The problem is that we don't typically put as much thought or effort into understanding the dynamics of a successful marriage as we do with work or sport. Have you noticed how often you talk to your buddies about what your favorite team should do to win more games? Have you really given that much thought to the success of your marriage?

The longer we are in relationships, the more we typically become complacent and just accept the status quo. Even if we do work hard to figure out what will make our marriage successful this week, it doesn't mean that those same rules will make the marriage a success the following week. As you know, life happens! Circumstances constantly change. Every week you may have a different scenario to evaluate in order to be successful. As a result, you need to constantly update your *playbook*—both at work and in your marriage.

A friend of mine, Edward, had a really good marriage with his wife, Irene. They had been married for seven years, with a three year old son, and still had a fun, flirtatious relationship with good communication. Then one day Eddy lost his job. Up until then, Eddy would call his wife during the day, and when he got home from work he would listen about her day as they prepared and served dinner. His wife looked forward to her husband coming home every evening so that she could share her day's stories. For her, Eddy was a great husband because he took such an interest in her life. She felt that he was her best friend.

But after he lost his job, Eddy's focus was almost all on himself. He spoke to Irene every day, but it was mostly focused on his own problems. Even when Irene started to talk about her life, Eddy managed to transition the conversation to his predicaments. How was he going to find a job? How did his interview go today? How will he contribute to paying the bills? Finding a job threw a wrench in their relationship as Eddy became singly focused on his career. Consequently, the dynamic of the relationship changed as the focus shifted from her to him.

Even though he was self-absorbed in finding work, Eddy needed to understand that his supportive wife still needed her daily dose of attention. Sure Irene understood the pressure Eddy was under to find a new position, but that didn't mean that Eddy had the right to totally ignore her.

The fun, caring, flirty Eddy was now the serious, depressed, grumpy Eddy. Even after he started working again, he didn't revert back to the husband that Irene married several years ago. Six months into his new job, Irene got so fed up with Eddy that she mentioned the possibility of divorce. This was the big wakeup call and resulted in them going to marriage counseling. Fortunately, they had enough love and understanding left in the gas tank to remedy the marriage and learn from their mistakes.

SUCCESS
REQUIRES EFFORT

You see, marriage, like work, requires a lot of attention to be successful. Neither one of you can take the other for granted. If you do, you may be out of both work and a marriage.

I have a favorite saying: "Your life can change in a second." What this means is that we can't expect things to remain as they are in the present moment. This can be interpreted both positively and negatively for most people. I always tell my children to enjoy things when they are good, because one day they may not be so great. For example, you may go years without any sickness and then one day wake up with a fever and the flu. You may love your job today, but tomorrow get a new manager who makes your life miserable. In just one second we can lose a job, become ill or even win the lottery. In life, we need to be prepared for change, yet never lose sight of the most important things. Your relationship with your wife may be the only safe harbor that you have in your life. She is the one person who truly cares about you and is there to support you day in and day out. You probably don't want to take her for granted.

Anytime you found success in life, it most likely took a lot of work to achieve it. There are no overnight sensations, no magic weight loss pills and no get rich quick schemes. Anything you do successfully takes work and discipline. If you play the violin in an orchestra, it took years to master the instrument. If you played baseball in high school, it took practicing every day to make the varsity team. The same applies to marriage.

I was invited to dinner at a friend's house and had the pleasure of meeting his parents. They were charming people, and we had a great time talking both before and after dinner. I got on the subject of marriage and raising a family with my friend's father, and he shared a story that really struck a chord with me.

They were not a wealthy couple. He was an

engineer and worked for many companies over the years. Often times he was out of work, and they lived a very difficult life. Yet the love and devotion he expressed for his wife was like nothing I had ever seen before. He shared that his wife had an equal love and admiration for him, too.

I asked what the secret was to the apparent success of their marriage, and he said that they worked at it every day. Through good times and bad, they approached life as a partnership and always supported each other. They never put each other down, criticized, nor ever complained about the other. They also made love to each other almost every night. He was rather proud of this last point!

CHANGE IN
MARRIAGE IS INEVITABLE

Have you thought about how your marriage has changed from the time you first met your wife to how it is today? Do you understand what your wife needs today, given changes (e.g. health, children, employment, family, etc.) that have occurred in your lives?

Have you stopped doing some of the basics of romance like opening doors for her, giving her compliments and saying that you love her? Have you stopped doing these things because you are frustrated with your marriage and lack of intimacy? Has your job gotten you so stressed that it is difficult for you to make your wife a priority? Have other things happened in your life that could impact the attention you pay to your wife?

These are some of the questions men need to ask themselves to become more aware of what is happening in their marriage.

A friend of mine, Jason, married his wife, Sara, a few years after college. He was from the Midwest and she was from the East Coast. Their marriage started out really great and lovingly, but Sara's mother passed away suddenly after just a few years of marriage. Needless to say, Sara was devastated by this sudden change in her life. The thought of not having her mother around any longer greatly impacted her personality and mood. As much as Jason was sympathetic to Sara's loss, his marriage nevertheless changed. It was no longer as much fun to be with Sara. Her interest in intimacy with Jason changed as she lost her playfulness. She told Jason that she was unable to stop thinking about her mother's sad state of affairs, and she continued to grieve for her.

Marriage is not a static environment that never changes. We as human beings are complicated creatures who are constantly exposed to new and different experiences that impact our beliefs and perspectives. For Jason and Sara, their marriage continued to be a challenge for many years. However, Jason remained committed to Sara and believed in their marriage vows of being with one another "through sickness and in health." Sara went for counseling to heal from the trauma, and Jason's support was rewarded with a wife who was able to accept and love again.

As we know, there are a multitude of circumstances that can easily impact the quality of a couple's relationship. The stories I have shared are just the tip of the iceberg. But no matter the situation, I have identified five behaviors that the husband should try incorporating into his marriage that will increase mutual happiness and also positively impact marital intimacy. I call the behaviors "The A-List of a *Sexy* Marriage".

Have you noticed that how much better you feel about yourself when your wife compliments you on your accomplishments or appearance? Doesn't it make you just love her even more for taking the time to recognize and appreciate you?

This goes both ways. She needs these things from you too!

Instead of feeling frustrated in your marriage, put your thoughts and energies into making your marriage great again. You married your wife for some really good reasons. Shall we stop for a moment to reflect on the reasons you selected your wife over all the other women in the world? Initially it was probably her physical appearance that caught your attention. Was it her hair, smile, eyes or figure? Then as you got to know her, what furthered the connection? Was it her sense of humor, intellect or caring personality? And didn't her mutual interest in you make you feel even more attracted to her? Remember the selfless nature of the relationship where you were both equally interested in making each other happy.

Regaining the "honeymoon status" of your marriage is not impossible and actually easier than you think. It will require some awareness and action on your part, but it will also pay great dividends.

WHAT IS A
SEXY MARRIAGE?

The phrase "*Sexy* Marriage" is included in the title of the book. What exactly does that mean?

I define a *sexy* marriage as a relationship that not only shares sex, but is also comprised of all the emotions and behaviors that make intimacy more loving, flirtatious, exciting and fun. Think about when you first met your wife and how exciting it was to see to her, talk to her and touch her. Remember how romantic and attentive you were? Remember how she responded to your actions with reciprocal attention and affection? THAT is what I define as a *sexy* marriage. Having sex is one thing, but for me the glass is only half full when you don't mix the emotions with the action. Sure life may be crazier compared to when you first met each other. You probably have more responsibilities, different pressures at work and possibly children to raise. But that does not mean that you can't rekindle those flames and keep the fire burning. Think of it like a camp fire: all you have to do is add some wood every day to keep it alive and burning strong. As we defined in the 1% Rule, focusing on your wife for just a few minutes a day can keep the proverbial fire alive. This is what differentiates sex from *sexy*!

I'd like to ask you right now, "What is stopping *you* from having a *sexy* marriage?" I know from personal experience that there are numerous things that can get in the way of a harmonious relationship. Is your wife unhappy with you because you aren't providing the financial security that she desires? Are there health issues that interfere with intimacy? Are there mundane things in your life that just cause tensions in the relationship (e.g. not remembering to take out the garbage, change the cat's litter box or pick up milk on the way home)?

I recall the time when I realized that I was living an emasculated lifestyle—I didn't feel like I was being treated like a man. It was not just my wife's fault; it was also mine for allowing it to be that way. Having read this far, you may be thinking that you feel this way too. But that's OK! It is far better to learn and adjust than to remain in an unhappy situation.

It is also very important that you go into this next section having mentally forgiven your wife for how she has treated you in the past. That was then, this is now! You need to enter this next section thinking positively that what you learn and integrate into your life can result in new responses and behaviors. These are solutions that can help move your marriage from a life of conflict to a life of harmony.

THE A-LIST OF
A *SEXY* MARRIAGE

The A-List of a *sexy* marriage consists of five classifications of communication or behavior that I have identified as being essential to a successful marriage. I believe that they are critical for turning an average marriage into a great marriage. As a whole, they address the emotions that should be incorporated into your daily life in order to give your wife happiness and promote feelings of love toward you. You may already do some of these things and find that only a slight modification to your behavior will do wonders, or you may realize that none of these things are currently being utilized at this moment in time. Either way, that is fine. We all need to start somewhere. Just realize that the perfect recipe includes all the behaviors. Leaving out just one may cause an imbalance in the relationship. It's like baking a cake and leaving out one of the ingredients: it just won't taste right.

Please consider that you must be honest in your communication. If you aren't, your wife will notice your insincerity and she will not open her heart for you. She will feel like you are patronizing her just to get sex.

I encourage you to start with a clean slate in your mind. Holding grudges for what she said or did to you in the past will just tarnish the benefits of moving forward and healing the relationship. When she sees that your new behavior doesn't include sarcasm or criticism, the relationship and intimacy will return in record time.

Here's the list. I suggest that you read them slowly and think about your current behavior as you read each one:

1. ACCEPT

It is important to accept your wife for who she is. As we all change throughout life, unconditionally accepting each other is a basic foundation of marriage. Let's face it: we all have things that we need to work on in order to be happy in our lives. Accepting means supporting each other throughout the process. For example, a female friend of mine had her own business that became unsuccessful. As you can imagine, she became very depressed due to her situation. Her loving husband accepted what happened to her and supported her throughout the transition. He continued to show loving support as she found a new career allowing her to regain confidence and loving emotions.

2. ADMIRE

Admiration (or respect) for your wife is key to loving her. Admiration is what enables a couple to care enough to work through problems and support each other during both good and bad times. Respect is first and foremost perceived by how intently you listen to your wife. A friend of mine dated his girlfriend for eight years throughout high school and college. Yet after they got married, the marriage ended in just one year. When I heard the news, I recall asking him what happened. His response was that they realized all they had in common was sex. They had no other interest in each other to hold things together. Admiration is the backbone of a solid relationship.

3. ADORE

Adoring your wife means that she has to feel the attraction and love that first brought you together. Adoring your wife entails giving her a big hug at the end of the day, looking into her eyes and telling her how much you love her. Adoring is her feeling that you love her more than anything else in the world. A female friend of mine has a loving husband that calls her throughout the day, and once a week he surprises her with something special (such as bath salts, a card or even a sexy night gown). She knows that her husband adores her! Adoring your wife is romancing your wife.

4. APPRECIATE

Appreciating your wife means you are grateful for the things that she does for you and the family. Appreciating means letting her know that you are thankful for even the smallest acts of kindness and generosity, and it means never taking her for granted. A friend of mine has three young children that keep his wife busy from breakfast to bedtime. He regularly tries to carve out time when he can watch the kids so that she can do her hobbies and socialize with girlfriends. He also gets babysitters regularly so they have time alone as a couple. This creates balance in their marriage, and they still have a great sex life.

5. ACTION

Action is critical for achieving anything in life. Without incorporating these behaviors into your daily routine, your relationship with your wife will not improve to the desired state of love and happiness. Taking action doesn't mean doing everything every day. It's fine to take baby steps at first to test the waters. Positive results will reinforce and reward your behavior.

A friend of mine, Rob, was in a long term marriage, running his own business and he also had over a dozen cats and dogs that he treated like children. When I visited his house one day, I talked to his wife Joyce about their marriage. She said that although she knew Rob loved her, he never did anything to make her feel special. It came as no shock to me when Rob complained to me that his sex life was stagnant. I suggested that he take Joyce out to a movie or dinner and that I would even stay home with the pets. He did, and it was the start of a renewed marriage. The key here is that you need to do something to elicit change. Don't just think it, do it!

If you incorporate the five behaviors already listed from The A-List into your daily life, you will receive a bonus "A": **Affection**. Your wife will see that you truly love and respect her, and in return, she may more than likely feel passionate toward you and reward you with affection. Your wife will feel more loving toward you, and you will see an improvement in how you communicate, touch, flirt and make love. I became friends with a young man that works in the produce department of a local grocery store. He has been married for three years, and one day we started talking about our lives and side projects. When I was telling him about my writing on relationships, he shared that he and his wife still have a great, affectionate marriage. I asked him why he thinks it has remained strong, and he said with a big smile on his face that it was because they still communicate, romance and make time to be together.

There is one more "A" that fits in this chapter, and that is being **Authentic** or sincere. I mentioned it at the beginning of the list, but feel it is important enough to mention it again. Sincerity about your feelings and behaviors supersedes all of the above. Behaving differently than how you truly feel is misleading and abusive to the other person. If your actions are not genuine, your insincerity will bubble to the surface and your marriage may fail in a heartbeat! A work colleague, Collin, dated a lot of women before he got married to a lady he romanced for two years. He was so used to winning over women, having sex and dumping them that when he found whom he thought was "Mrs. Right", he didn't realize that he was still using a lot of insincere behavior in his relationship with her. His fiancée was so focused on the wedding day that she never saw through this—until it was too late. They got married, then unfortunately realized that the marriage was not grounded on authenticity. The marriage was annulled after a few months.

When you read "The A-List of a *Sexy* Marriage", what is the first thing that comes to mind where you possibly fall short?

Don't be shy or judgmental of yourself. We all have areas to work on. Even the best marriages could use some review in a few areas.

Let's say that your wife feels that you are a really good provider and that you always put her first when it comes to material needs. But what if she also feels disconnected romantically because you don't show her that you adore her? As a result, wouldn't your intimacy suffer? What if you were to start expressing how attracted you are to her, how much you love her hugs and how her smile makes you melt? Do you think that would make a difference in your relationship?

What if she felt that you adored her, yet she didn't feel that you were very supportive of her career? Do you think that listening to her talk about work and being genuinely interested in her accomplishments would make her feel admired by you?

My brother-in-law Mike had been married to my sister Debbie for over forty years. Every evening after work, Mike listened to Debbie talk about her day as a school teacher. I noticed how appreciative she felt toward her husband taking a genuine interest in her work and accomplishments. I gathered that this contributed to their wonderful relationship and intimacy. When I say intimacy, I have no idea what went on in their bedroom. But when I saw them watching TV together in the evening, they usually were hugging with their arms wrapped around each other. It always brought a sense of happiness to my heart.

There may be a number of areas in your marriage where you have been consistently falling short. The great thing now is that when you recognize what needs improvement, it is then so easy to make adjustments and *immediately* see positive results in your marriage.

Some behaviors may be neglected due to temporary things happening in your life. For example, you may have a major project at work that takes an inordinate amount of time and focus. As a result, you may not be showing your wife how much you admire and adore her as she has come to expect. But if you review the list and realize that you are falling short here and there, wouldn't it be great to spend a few minutes giving your wife what she needs? And how about even letting your wife know what you realized? Sometimes telling her that you screwed up and admitting your flaws can be perceived as a positive thing. I bet that she would be more understanding of your situation if she knows how much you care about her and want her in your life.

A friend of mine, Nolan, met his wife, Laura, right after college. He is an engineer with a Ph.D. degree from an Ivy League school. She is a social worker. They dated for a few years and had a lot in common, including science and movies. They would go to lectures all the time and spend many hours sipping wine while talking about what they just experienced. They never really reviewed their aspirations before they got married as they were busy working, maintaining their own apartments and otherwise just enjoying each other's company on weekends.

After they got married, Laura discovered that Nolan was not very motivated to make money. This really upset her, as she automatically thought in the back of her head that Nolan would be a good provider. She just assumed that anyone with a Ph.D. would make a lot of money.

This, as you can imagine, caused a lot of conflict and disappointment in the relationship. Laura lost her acceptance and admiration for Nolan, as her expectations were not being met. Nolan, conversely, lost his feelings of adoring Laura. As a couple, they had three A's that were not being addressed.

Fortunately Nolan cared enough for Laura and thought that this problem could be worked out. He suggested that they take action, the fifth A, and dedicated a weekend talking about their problems and how they could resolve them. Their conversations, which included everything from intellectual, emotional and physical aspects, allowed them to gain an objective understanding of the situation and create a plan for regaining mutual respect. They started with accepting who each person was, and then they realized all the good things that they had as a couple. Acceptance led to a renewed appreciation of the wonderful things they each brought to the relationship.

Going back to the Super Bowl analogy, having a happy and fulfilling marriage is all about sticking to the basics—the A-List of a *sexy* marriage. If one forgets to address the A-List in their marriage, then they shouldn't expect to win the game or have a great relationship.

In the back of the book I share with you a brief exercise to evaluate how you can better communicate with your wife. I first give you examples of things you can say to your wife that address all four of the "A's". There is space to write down statements that best suit your wife and your marriage today. After you incorporate these statements, it will be great to see how your wife reacts to the changes you made in your communication towards her. Notice if she shows you more affection, like touching you more, or gives you a kiss and says "thank you".

Just remember, what she needs today may be different than what she needs tomorrow.

Circumstances may change that require different focus. For example, today your wife may be very confident and not need you to focus on how much you admire her. But what if something happened at her job where she now feels insecure? She may now need more Admiration reinforcement where you tell her how talented and underappreciated she is at work. Review the exercise periodically to reevaluate her needs and the focus of your communication. Over time, you will start to strategically address her needs without even consciously thinking about it as this process will become second nature to you.

THE HAPPY
AND
SEXY QUIZ

THE SCHLOSS LEAD IN

1. *Understand where you stand in your marriage today*
2. *Understand what your wife needs to be happy*
3. *Realize that small change can earn big premiums*

"Everything's easy once you know how to do it!"

Now that you have discovered how important it is to give your wife attention via the 1% Rule and reminded yourself of the behaviors women need from the A-List, let's take a moment to evaluate your current state of affairs.

This is not a test to measure if you are a good or bad husband, but rather to benchmark where you are today so that you can monitor progress in the future. We all have things to work on in relationships just like we do at work and with other activities. It is recognizing what we do well and what areas need improvement that are critical to having a happy and sexy marriage. If you were a running back playing football and your offensive line wasn't creating openings, then how would you ever expect to advance the ball closer to the goal line?

I must say that I am not a big fan of tests. So I purposely designed this quiz to be simple, fast and easy. It is a straight forward way to recognize how well you are currently addressing the A-List of *your marriage.*

I also want to preface that you be totally honest in how you answer these mere 10 questions. As I stated, there is no judging here. We are simply creating an awareness of your marriage today and noting where you can make changes for future improvement.

For the following 10 questions, please answer "Yes" or "No" if you perform these behaviors on a regular basis, or as otherwise noted in the question. Feel free to circle your answers here or use The Man's Secret Notes section provided for you at the back pages of the book.

1. When you go out with your wife, do you always open the car door for her, as well as other doors?   Yes or No

2. Do you tell your wife that you love her every day? Yes or No

3. When your wife talks to you, do you always give her your undivided attention? Yes or No

4. Do you support your wife in achieving her goals and dreams? Yes or No

5. Do you surprise your wife every few weeks with something special like flowers, cupcakes, candy or a card?   Yes or No

6. Do you show appreciation to your wife weekly for what she does at work or around the home?   Yes or No

7. When your wife is going through health or work problems that may impact your

relationship and intimacy, do you support her unconditionally?   Yes or No

8. When your wife is upset with something you have done, do you talk to her instead of running from the discussion?   Yes or No

9. When you have sex with your wife, are you selfless and focused on pleasuring her first? Yes or No

10. Do you flirt with your wife and make her laugh every day?   Yes or No

Now total up the number of "Yes" and "No" responses individually.

If you answered affirmatively on five or fewer questions, then I am excited for you because this information will be extremely valuable for you in improving your relationship. You probably did a lot of these things for your wife when you were dating or newly married, but the trials and tribulations of life may have resulted in you paying less attention to the things she needs from you to feel and share love. That is OK! It is actually awesome that you are here right now. Don't you feel empowered that you are investing your time and energy to discover ways to have a better marriage? As for most men, it really doesn't take much work or time to see a big change in your wife's feelings and behavior toward you.

If you answered affirmatively to six or seven questions, you are doing very well in how you communicate with your wife. Looks like you just need to tweak a few things here or there in order to take your relationship to the next level. Perhaps you are addressing four of the five areas really well and just have to focus on one or two in order for your wife to think you are the best husband ever!

If you answered affirmatively to eight to ten questions, you are doing a great job communicating with your wife. If she isn't responding lovingly toward you, then there may be other issues—physical or emotional—that are preventing her from being a loving and sexy wife. Do you know what they could be? Have you talked to her about them?

The important things to recognize are that your wife needs to feel adored, admired, appreciated and accepted. She also needs to see that you are taking positive action toward totally opening her heart for you. If just one thing is missing, there will be an imbalance.

For example, you may appreciate and admire your wife. However, if you don't adore or romance her, she may miss the thrill and excitement of being swept off her feet. This will cause her to not be as willing to share herself with you.

Conversely, the woman may actually be accepted and adored by her husband, but he may not take the action to demonstrate it. Hence, she may not *feel* the romance in the marriage and therefore be less inclined to share intimacy with her husband.

I met a gentleman on a plane during a business trip. His name was Isaac, and he was an engineer. He married his wife a little over two years prior to me meeting him but already felt that some things were strained in his marriage. He said that he adored his wife and frequently told her how much he appreciated her support and love. But he, being such a practical man, missed the mark when it came to romantic behavior as he always felt a little clumsy in that category. But now that the marriage had settled in, his wife felt like romance was an important precursor to sex. Even though he satisfied many of the behaviors on the A-List, his lack of romance was a deterrent to his wife opening up to him sexually.

A business acquaintance of mine, Mark, had accepted a new position within his company. He was totally immersed in his career, as well as impressed by his new level of responsibility because he was now managing quite a few people. It was surely an ego boost. Mark continued to romance his wife and make her feel secure in their relationship. However, he was so self-focused that he neglected talking to his wife about her own career and life aspirations. In other words, she felt neglected because he didn't acknowledge her career the same way he did in the past. Whenever she would come home and start talking about her job situation, Mark quickly switched the conversation to a similar situation at his job. As a result, his wife did not feel as close to him. Their relationship was strained.

You see, the four A's of adore, appreciate, accept and admire are like the footings at four corners of a building. For the woman to be selfless to her husband, she needs a solid foundation of feelings from her man. If one piece of the foundation is missing, the temple of marriage can easily crumble.

If you look at the list of ten questions that you answered above, the first two speak to showing your wife that you adore her. Numbers three and four relate to how you admire her. Five and six demonstrate appreciation. Seven and eight refer to acceptance. The last two relate to taking action. Do you now have a better sense of areas that need attention so as to make your wife happy?

SMALL CHANGE PAYS
BIG MARRIAGE DIVIDENDS

I firmly believe that all it takes for a woman to reopen her heart to her husband is a minor change in behavior. We always hear that men are simple and women are complicated. But in reality, my experience in speaking with women is that they'd be really happy if their husbands made even minor behavioral changes that outwardly expressed love. If you make these changes, I bet that you will see an instantaneous change in how your wife reacts to you.

I suggest that you re-read the A-List chapter every few days to remind yourself of the things that your wife needs from you. Perhaps even make a photocopy of the pages and carry them around with you. Then, every two weeks come back and take the quiz again. I have read that if you do the same thing over and over for three weeks that it will become a new habit. That is the goal we are shooting for here.

But, take it slow and steady. Monitor your wife's reactions to your new actions too. Be sure that you are sincere and consistent. It is this continuity that will lead her to believe that you can and want to change!

As we all know, no marriage is perfect. It is the couples who best understand and address the behaviors of a happy, fulfilling relationship who are able to remain dedicated to each other.

SCHLOSS' LIST OF "101 WAYS TO HAVE A *SEXY* MARRIAGE"

THE SCHLOSS LEAD IN

1. *Reactivating chemistry in the marriage*
2. *Pay close attention to her reactions*
3. *Make it a lot of FUN!*

> "Women need to feel connected to have sex. Men need to have sex to feel connected"

Having a sexy marriage is not just about having sex. It is about your wife feeling appreciated, adored, accepted and admired by you, her man. It is about her having the same feelings of respect and love for you that she had when you first started dating. It is about being flirty, romantic, and showing her how much you love her on a day to day basis.

With the divorce rate of second marriages being even higher than first marriages, don't think that the grass is necessarily always greener by leaving and finding someone else. You selected your wife because you had a special chemistry. That chemistry may be suppressed right now, but take my word, it is far better to try and fix your relationship than to go through a terrible divorce. Your problems could be the same or *even worse* when you settle down with someone else. Divorce may sound like an easy exit strategy, but I would hope that you make it your action of last resort. It is far better to focus on having a sexy life with the woman you married!

Now that you know your wife needs certain types of communication from you, let's get even more specific. What things can you say or do for your wife that will make her have positive, warm feelings for you again? To have that sexy marriage, you need to address her sensuality using all of her senses. She needs to feel connected to you via touch, smell, sight, taste and sound. Think about it: what can you do to give your wife feelings of love by using all of her senses?

Remember when you first met your wife and how she got goose bumps of excitement when you touched her? Remember the sounds of passion she made when you kissed her? Remember how you spoke to her using the sexy tone of your voice? How about how each of you made a special effort to be clean, smell fresh and have delicious kisses? And let's not forget how you spent extra time grooming yourself and picking out clothes when you were going to meet her.

The following list of "101 Ways to Have a Sexy Marriage" addresses all of the senses. You don't have to spend a lot of money to have a sexy marriage. In fact, the most meaningful things you can do for your wife do not require any money at all. I have seen other lists of how to romance a woman including things like lavish trips. However, it doesn't mean that she would feel any sexier toward you if you did them.

I have learned from experience that it is the day to day things that mean the most to a woman. This does not mean that you don't wine and dine her on occasion. But as I have expressed earlier, it is daily consistency that matters the most in the world—especially to a woman. If you and your wife have built a great relationship due to daily expressions of love and caring, then a trip to her favorite place would further reinforce your love for each other. But you can't expect a short-term vacation to heal long-term problems in a relationship.

As I state in my quotation at the top of the chapter, "women need to feel connected to have sex, and men need sex to feel connected". As shared in the chapter on power, women have control over a man's sexual satisfaction. And the way that the man earns love and admiration from a woman is by addressing her emotional needs first. When the man is selfless to a woman, she is selfless and loving in return. But the laws of nature make it that the man has the responsibility, and must take the initiative, to first create the loving, secure environment. And the interesting thing is the man that does this receives love, and sex, in return. And the more the man has wonderful, loving intimacy with his woman, the more he feels connected to her and wants to please her even more. In a truly wonderful, loving marriage, there is no thought of cheating or wandering, because the man knows in his heart that he has hit the jackpot of life. As the actor Paul Newman once quoted, when asked if he ever thought about cheating on his wife, actress Joanne Woodward: "Why fool around with hamburger when you have steak at home?" Well said!

FROM MARRIED ROOMMATES TO INTIMATE LOVERS

A friend of mine, Eric, told me that his marriage was stagnant for a number of years. He and his wife, Liz, were so busy working and raising the kids that they became more like roommates. He was also challenged at work and did not make the type of money he needed to contribute to a comfortable family lifestyle. These issues turned what should have been a love nest in their bedroom into a battleground. Eric had a strong desire for sex with his wife, but he didn't create the right environment for Liz to feel sexy towards him. Needless to say, their marriage was on the rocks.

So I shared with Eric some ideas from my "101 Ways to Have a Sexy Marriage" and Eric started to do some of them. At first, Liz was surprised to see his renewed interest in romancing her. She thought that he was just giving her "lip service" to try and get laid! He told her that he truly loved her and was sorry that he was neglectful of their relationship and her needs. As

Eric continued to consistently be attentive to his wife, the love and romance once again blossomed for both of them. Were they having sex every day—of course not! But they let each other know that they loved each other every day. Their intimacy was not just fostered through sex but also through showing love to each other both inside as well as outside of the bedroom. Brings tears to my eyes!

Take your time reviewing the list, and note some things that you think will work for you. Remember, the key is to take action. You may see suggestions that spark other ideas that may work for you and your lady. Once you find something that really strikes a chord with your wife, think of other similar things that you can do with or for her. Consciously think of which senses she responds to the most. Even though we want to utilize all of the senses when being sexy, everyone has a specific sense that is more dominant and generates more of a response. Some women will react more positively to food, others to music or outdoor activities.

If you find your wife really enjoys dancing and it creates an atmosphere of fun and romance, try to take her dancing once a month. You can always find a live band or DJ on a Friday or Saturday night. If she likes romantic movies, rent a chick flick on the TV every few weeks, and serve popcorn with wine or champagne. If she likes art, every town has an art museum or galleries to enjoy for an afternoon. Keeping it simple is the way to go.

THE **SCHLOSS** LIST OF
101 Ways to
Have a Sexy Marriage

1. When you are sitting in close proximity to your life, but not right next to her, send a text message to her phone stating that you love her. Then wait for her response. When she replies back positively, send another text or two- having some fun with the *game*. You will hear her laughing as she reads your messages. Then after a few exchanges go over to her, give her a big kiss and tell her how much you love her!

2. Use words of endearment. Have you stopped calling your wife "sweetie," "baby" or some other pet name? Reactivate those sincere words of love, and see how she reacts to you.

3 "The Schloss Buckle" – (a favorite for most). When you go to the car with your wife, don't just open the door for her and then immediately go to your side of the car. Instead, after she sits down, grab her seat belt and reach across her body to buckle her in. Then give her a big hug and kiss and say "I love you".

4 Go to bed at the same time. This sounds so simple, but it is very important to share time together in bed—the most intimate place in your house.

5 When you are with your wife in public but you are also so talking to other people, make a loud enough comment about how special your wife is so that she can hear it too. It can be about a skill she has, what a wonderful mother she is, or even how supportive she is as a wife. Make eye contact with her and wink!

6 Take your wife to the movies and sit in the back row of the theater so that you can hug and kiss. This is not just for teenagers!

7   When you go to a restaurant, try and find a table where you can sit next to each other. There are many things you can do above and below the table to show love and build anticipation for when you get home

8   Hold hands in public, and don't forget to kiss her hand too. It is so romantic and a great way to stay emotionally connected to your wife.

9   Show lots of PDA (public displays of affection) when you are in public areas and you feel comfortable (e.g. holding hands, kissing and even grabbing her butt).

10   Buy cinnamon, and have it in the house. Have cinnamon potpourri or a cinnamon candle in your bedroom. Vanilla is also a great scent for the senses. These are considered aphrodisiacs.

11   Call you wife during the day and tell her how much you miss her and can't wait to hug her when you get home. Don't talk about sex unless she starts to do it first, otherwise you will come across as just wanting sex. Remember, this is *all* about HER!

12   Break the Saturday night routine and do something that you haven't done in years like dancing or going to a concert.

13   Prepare a bubble bath for her either at home or at a hotel. If the tub is large enough, after a few minutes ask if you can join in. Then have fun with the bubbles! P.S. if the bathtub has jets, just use them for a second or you will have bubbles all over the floor!

14   Plan a night in bed watching a chick flick of her choice. Romantic movies bring out romantic emotions!

15   Sing to her on the phone or in person. Women love to be serenaded, no matter how bad your voice or how poorly you carry a tune. They just love be romanced, and this is a great way to do it.

16   Go up to your wife and whisper in her ear how much you love her.

17   Plan in advance, like finding a baby sitter for the kids or a dog walker, and tell your wife to pack a bag because you are taking her to a hotel for the night.

18 Go for a walk in the rain, then shower together when you get back.

19 Cook your wife dinner. Women love it when men take the initiative to cook for them. They find it very romantic and masculine. Don't forget the candles!

20 Fully listen to your wife for 10 minutes right when you come home. Be present! Let her tell you about her day at work, the kids, and social matters with her friends and family.

21 Stay physically fit. You want your wife to find you attractive so that she wants to rip your clothes off, right?! Find time in your busy schedule to do some physical activity every day or at least three times a week for 20 minutes. Walking, running, biking, swimming—anything where you can raise your heart rate and sweat a bit. Don't forget to throw in some pushups and sit ups to make the exterior as attractive as the interior (check with your doctor before you start any new physical activity).

22   Approach your wife from behind and whisper sweet things in her ear. Let her know how lucky you are to have her in your life.

23   Give your wife a back or shoulder massage. This could occur when she is sitting at a chair or in bed. Start by rubbing her shoulders, and see if she moans about how good it feels. If you get positive feedback, ask her if she would like to lie down on her stomach for a massage. Ask her where she wants you to concentrate your efforts. Make this all about her!

24   Write her a handmade card telling her how much you love her. Use crayons or other things around the house to draw red hearts as well as big X's and O's. You don't have to be an artist. She will love the effort you made!

25   Cook dinner together. Preparing food and drinking a little wine together are very romantic activities. It also gives you many opportunities to laugh and touch each other.

26 Grab her in your arms like a man. Look her in the eyes and tell her how much you love her.

27 If your wife has long hair, brush her hair out of her face with your hand and give her a look of love when you do it.

28 Book her a massage at a salon. This gives her time alone to be pampered. She will also love telling her friends about what a wonderful husband you are!

29 Bring home dinner. Call her at noon and tell her that you are taking care of dinner tonight.

30 Arrange to send the children to the grandparents, cousins or friends for a night or weekend. The kids will love it, and you will get some quality time together.

31 Hire someone to help with things around the house, such as a housekeeper to clean the house twice a month.

32 When you have evening plans with your wife, call her in the afternoon and tell her

that you have a "hot date" tonight. She will most likely reply, "Really, with whom?" Then you reply by describing your wife and her best attributes. It could go something like this: "Oh, I have a dinner date with this adorable, sexy woman that I met about 15 years ago. She has the best smile, delicious lips and is so much fun to talk to."

33 Send flirty text messages throughout the day. This will show her that you love her as well as build anticipation for when you get home.

34 Make a date to watch her favorite TV program together every week. Make a bowl of popcorn, put your feet up on the ottoman and snuggle while you watch.

35 Leave a love note on the windshield of her car, or somewhere that you know she will find it during the day, when you depart for work in the morning.

36 Hug her all the time, even if it's for just a second (e.g. like when passing by her in the kitchen to get food on the table for the family).

37 Bring home chocolates or a delicacy that she really enjoys, such as a cupcake in her favorite flavor.

38 Bringing home flowers to your wife on a Friday night is a great way to start the weekend!

39 Make love to your wife facing her while hugging her as tight as you can. She will hug back. Stare into her eyes. It will bring out a lot of the emotions you share for each other.

40 Be a good listener. Sometimes a woman just needs her man to "just listen" without providing any solutions or quick fixes. Also listen closely to what may be unspoken.

41 Do something together that neither one of you has done before. Experiencing it together for the first time can build lasting memories and make your relationship stronger.

42 Always open doors for your wife. It is one of the most basic expressions of chivalry.

43 Take her to a comedy club. You know how women always say that they love a guy whom makes them laugh. Laughter is an aphrodisiac, so enjoy it together.

44 Play a fun game at home such as Scrabble, Monopoly or even take out Twister and see if you can get your bodies tangled together.

45 Do a crossword puzzle together. This is great as you get to sit close together, touch, and be a little competitive—but also compliment her or her answers! These are great for at home as well as when traveling on a plane or train.

46 Bring home some candles and tell your wife that you would like to make love to her by candlelight.

47 Go spend a day at the beach together. Spend time in the water touching and hugging. When lying in the sun, be sure you are close enough that you can hold hands. Then, finish with a beachside dinner on the way home.

48   Go for a picnic. Pack a blanket, a bottle of wine, cheese and crackers. Find a site with a beautiful view, such as at the top of a hill overlooking a river. Relax and enjoy each other's company.

49   Take her for a day cruise. Do you live near a river or lake? Go for a two or three hour boat ride. This is very romantic, and she will appreciate the carefree time away from home.

50   Go for a bike ride together. Riding bikes is great fun. Pack some snacks and find a beautiful place to stop, take in the views and enjoy each other's company.

51   Go for ice cream. There is something special about ice cream and how it soothes the soul. Have a little fun and look your wife in the eyes when you are licking your cone. Maybe she will do the same for you!

52   Pick up a bag of her favorite coffee, tea or snack. She will really appreciate the thoughtfulness.

53 Role play. If your wife is receptive to this, it can be very erotic and awaken fantasies in the relationship. What roles would you suggest? How about you both drive to a bar separately and you *pick her up*! Then take her home for some fun! However, don't forget that you left a car at the bar or restaurant.

54 Pretend it is your first date again. Tell your wife to meet you at the place you first met. Then, role play like you are meeting for the first time.

55 Take your wife clothes shopping for the afternoon. Sit patiently while she selects clothes, and ask her to give you a fashion show while she tries things on.

56 Write down all the things you love about her, roll it up, seal it with a ribbon, and then give it to her as a gift. She will treasure and save it for sure.

57 Compliment your wife on her appearance: her figure, clothes, jewelry, even her perfume!

58 Compliment your wife on her shoes or handbag. For many women, shoes and handbags are fashion statements of the highest order.

59 Recognize when your wife gets her hair done, nails painted, new clothes, etc. Never criticize the cost, as these are essential components of her femininity.

60 Tell your wife how sexy she is every week. Let her know that you still find her attractive and desirable.

61 Compliment her on the food she prepares for you. It shows appreciation, and a woman loves to please her man with food.

62 Have flowers delivered to the home just for her.

63 Write a love note and put it in her purse or work bag.

64 Surprise her with cleaning the house when she is running errands or out with friends.

65   Give your wife a foot massage. She will melt like butter!

66   When you are in public, make a point of not looking at other women. Give her your total attention. She may feel dismissed or unattractive if you are distracted.

67   Go to an amusement park together. Go on fast, scary rides and have her hold onto you for security.

68   Hand feed your wife things she enjoys like grapes or strawberries. Tease her with the food; rub it on her lips before putting it in her mouth. It can be very erotic and sensual.

69   Go for a canoe or paddle boat ride. Being on the water and in the sun is fun as well as relaxing—and a nice change of scenery.

70   Visit a city for a day. Take a carriage ride if they have one. Stop at a nice bar. Eat at an outdoor café.

71   Encourage her to have a girls' night out. She will really appreciate you breaking her routine.

72   Make a fire in the fireplace, spread a blanket on the floor, open a bottle of wine, have some finger foods and enjoy the glowing warmth of the fire together.

73   Dress yourself nicely; be well groomed for your wife. She will be turned on by your appearance.

74   Use a non-sexual touch on her arms, neck, shoulders. She will close her eyes and purr like a kitten!

75   When it is time for bed, go to the bedroom together and tell your wife that *you* want to undress her. Do it very slowly, being sure to often look her in the eyes. Watch as the magic unfolds.

76   Have your wife sit on your lap. Hug her from behind, rub her shoulders, play with her hair, and whisper sweet things to her.

77   Surprise her by coming home early. Go do an activity like a walk together or dinner and a movie.

78   Make an effort to say goodbye to her an extra time. Go back in the house after leaving and say that you need one more kiss!

79   Surprise her with breakfast in bed.

80   Tell her how happy you are to have her in your life.

81   Buy her something that she will use that causes her to think about you all the time, such as a key chain or cell phone case that you picked out for her.

82   Buy her a gift card for her favorite store.

83   Spontaneously stop at a hotel and get a room for a few hours.

84   Buy her some bath salts for her to enjoy and relax with after a long day with the kids.

85   Make an extra effort to be nice to her parents and friends. She will really appreciate it.

86   Make her a photo album of things the two of you have done together. This is really easy now to do online.

87 Take silly photos at a photo booth or on your cell phone, and put the photos on the refrigerator.

88 Write her a poem and send it to her in the mail. No emails, please!

89 Propose to her for a second time. Find a favorite, romantic spot and then take her out for dinner.

90 Buy her helium balloons that say, "I Love You."

91 Carry her over the threshold when you return home one evening. Just don't hurt your back!!!

92 When she talks to you, stop what you are doing and give her your undivided attention

93 Buy her massage lotion, and tell her that you would love to use it on her.

94 Buy new silk sheets for the bed. Women love beautiful fabrics (remember the sense of touch!), so this will be something greatly appreciated—and anticipated to use with you.

95   Stop together on the way home at an adult store and find something fun to use in bed that evening.

96   Buy her a CD of her favorite artist, and then listen to it together.

97   Spend an afternoon visiting art museums or art galleries. This is a great chance to be close, activate the senses and talk about things besides your personal life.

98   Check off something on her bucket list. Have you talked to her recently about things she wants to do in her life? Make a note of them, and see which ones you can do.

99   Go grocery shopping together. It can be fun picking out produce together and planning menus while walking the aisles of the store.

100   Help your wife fold the laundry. She will appreciate the extra effort to lighten her load.

101   Surprise her by cleaning her car, both inside and out. Either wash it yourself or

take it to the car wash. She will be delighted by your thoughtfulness.

I shared this list with a work colleague recently. He got back to me a week later and said that he "got ten times the amount of attention in return" from using just a few of the ideas on the list. You can too!

Keep a mental or written list of how your wife reacts to your actions. Be creative and try other things that you think will elevate her sense of love toward you. Make it fun!

You will feel like you are dating and romancing your wife the same way as when you first met. Ah, the rushes of adrenaline and endorphin reactivation are some of the best feelings in life. You may even want to create your own list of 101 Ways!

I also encourage you to share my website, **www.mantomantalks.com**, with your friends. On the home page I offer a free download of an excerpt from this list so that they can enhance their marriage too!

4 STRATEGIES TO GET SEX BACK IN YOUR MARRIAGE

THE SCHLOSS LEAD IN

1. *Why your wife isn't reciprocating*
2. *Actions you can take to regain sex in the marriage*
3. *Schloss' 10 Do's and Don'ts List*

"Sleeping lonely alone is better than sleeping lonely with someone else"

If by now you are finding that the *new you* has not improved your intimacy or love life, then it may be time to take more drastic action in your marriage. If you feel that you have truly made the effort to understand the needs of your wife and have selflessly worked to give her what she needs in the marriage, then it may be time to take actions to another level.

Your marriage may have been in a rut for so long that change *may* seem virtually impossible. Perhaps your wife has so much resentment that she is callous to the thought of giving you what you want. Sometimes we need to take stronger action to force change in our lives. It's like going to the gym and doing the same routine every day without seeing much bodily change, but then you start working with a trainer who pushes you beyond your usual routine. Bam! That is when you start to see a noticeable improvement!

Have you noticed that you can tell your wife a hundred million times that if she doesn't have sex with you then you will leave her, cheat on her or even divorce her—yet these threats do not work. She more than likely will still not have sex with you regularly. Why is that? It's likely to be one of four common reasons: 1) She doesn't believe you; 2) She doesn't think you are man enough to follow through; 3) She just doesn't care about sex; or 4) She hasn't thought through the repercussions.

We all go through times in our lives where our libido is repressed for one reason or another. However, we also have a responsibility to be selfless and keep our partners happy—have you treated your wife with love and care as reviewed in the 1% Rule? Do you feel that your wife *doesn't* have any major psychological or physical conditions that could be affecting her interest in sex? If yes to one or both of these questions, then it may be time to change your strategy!

Have you heard the phrase, "Actions speak louder than words"? I am sure you have! What this means is that you actually have to take action to enable change.

How do we take action?

There are four strategies the man can pursue in order to get his wife to have sex with him again.

THE FOUR STRATEGIES

STRATEGY 1

The least aggressive action you may consider to regain your power, and sex, is to stop showing any interest in intimacy. That's right: no more begging, pleading or groping for sex.

You need to continue being a loving, caring husband. Just stop any sexually forward behavior. When you go to bed give your wife a quick hug and kiss, tell her that you love her, roll to your side of the bed and go to sleep.

It won't take long for your wife to wonder what the heck is going on, and it also won't take long for her to start paying attention to you again. Your behavior will start a myriad of thoughts in her head of potentially adverse effects, including that you may be thinking of cheating or a divorce.

If she asks you why you are acting this way, just tell her that you are tired of being rejected and sexually frustrated. Then say that you would like to go to sleep. Bam! First action taken!

If your wife really loves you and is not interested in ending the marriage, she will probably make the moves *on you* to have sex. First step to getting the power back!

My friend, Chris, was a really good husband and father. His wife, Barbara, complained that she was always too tired to have sex as she was busy working, raising the kids and keeping the house in order. But Chris did a lot around the house to help Barbara, and he even hired a housekeeper to lessen her load. But no matter how much Chris romanced his wife or expressed his interest in loving her both emotionally and physically, Barbara was not receptive to his advances.

Chris realized that there needed to be a wakeup call to break the habit. He was so sexually frustrated that he decided to stop pursuing sex with his wife. Why keep trying every night and getting rejected? So when Chris got into bed with Barbara, he stopped begging and groping. He just gave her a hug, told her he loved her and wished her a good night's sleep.

After a few nights of this, Barbara was perplexed by Chris' new behavior. She asked him if everything was okay, as she noticed things were different. She was starting to show some concern because his change of behavior may have an impact on her marriage and lifestyle. Could he be thinking about a divorce, cheating or engaging in some other detrimental behavior?

This change of behavior, as well as Barbara's concern over its potential impact, opened the door for communication. Chris now had the full attention of his wife to listen to his perspective. If she started to interrupt, he firmly told her that this was his time to voice his grievances about their marriage. Chris now had some leverage to *negotiate* a better marriage. By not showing any interest in sex, Chris took back some of the power that Barbara wielded over him. It opened her eyes that for the marriage to work, both partners need to be satisfied in the relationship.

STRATEGY 2

If the first stage doesn't work and your wife shows no concern for your change in behavior, nor empathy for your position, then we move to the second stage.

Remember that we are looking to take actions to evoke change. The next action you may consider is physically moving to another bedroom or sleeping on the couch.

Bam! You have taken action again and that should get her thinking even more seriously that you may leave or file for divorce. You are showing her again, via action, that you mean business. You don't even have to mention any of your sexual frustration. She already knows it, believe me.

I was talking to a guy on the train one day about his marriage, and he shared this story. Fred was in a bad marriage where his wife had not had sex with him in months. He shared that he and his wife constantly fought, and the fights got worse if he ever showed any affection toward her. He figured that his sexual advances triggered her being even more belligerent toward him. I asked how he treated his wife, and Fred said that he continued to be respectful, assist with things around the house and tell her that he loved her.

It has gotten to the point where sleeping next to his wife and being sexually rejected was too painful. Fred said that he would try to caress his wife, but her rejections resulted in him curling up into the fetal position in bed and crying himself to sleep. Then the day came when Fred couldn't take it anymore, and he moved into the guest bedroom. He figured that being lonely while sleeping alone was better than being lonely while sleeping with someone else.

Bam! Fred took some action to get some power back into his life! He now removed himself from the temptation of groveling for affection and sex. He chose to separate himself from that emasculating situation by removing himself from the marital bedroom.

After a few nights, Fred's wife came and knocked on the guest bedroom door where Fred was sleeping. She begged him to come back to the marital bedroom. At first Fred refused by saying that he was really hurt and was not interested in getting back into a situation where he was rejected by his wife. The next night his wife knocked on his door again and without saying a word started to rub his shoulders, caress him and proceeded to make love to her husband for the first time in months.

Fred said that this didn't fix the problem, but it sure felt great to make love to his wife again. What this did accomplish, however, was it opened the channels of intimacy and allowed them to talk more lovingly about their problems.

STRATEGY 3

If the prior two strategies didn't work, perhaps getting some space away from your wife would be healthy for the both of you in order to think about your situation. You may want to stay at a friend's or family member's house for a few nights. If you choose this strategy, just be honest, and let your wife know where you are going and why you are doing it. Then see her reaction. Just please don't be a *no show* for a number of days. That would not be good.

You need to be careful here as some states may consider leaving the family residence as abandonment depending on the number of days that you stay away. You may want to check with an attorney before taking this action. Also, it is noteworthy to say that you know your situation better than anyone else and seeking the advice of professionals, such as doctors and or attorneys, is always best prior to making this kind of decision. At the end of the day, this is your responsibility and your call. We often don't know what we don't know and it is a good idea to gain as much knowledge as possible, particularly when it is a family matter.

STRATEGY 4

If you find that all of the prior suggestions don't work and that your marriage is still on the rocks, then you may want to consider another type of action.

Sometimes, women have hormonal imbalances or a medical condition that prevents them from having a sex drive or finding it pleasurable. It may be worthwhile to see a doctor. Some women actually find sex painful, yet they don't communicate that to their spouse. Instead they just reject their partner. No matter what it is, continue to be the man, communicate and take action to solve or resolve your marriage problem(s).

By taking action in your marriage, you will feel like the man in your marriage again. You have probably been saying "yes dear" for so long that it will feel wonderful standing up for yourself. Working proactively to get what you want and need in your relationship is very empowering.

Remember why your wife wanted to get married in the first place. The woman wanted to get married for the purpose of comfort and security. By taking back the power, you are threatening these creature comforts. As a result, you are reclaiming respect but in a caring and loving way.

Schloss'
10 Do's and Don'ts List:
Keys for Success

There are some very important things you should remember at this junction. Here are some important "do's" and "don'ts" that merit your consideration, based on my conversations with other men:

The Do's

1. Do tell your wife that you still love her as much as the day you married her.

2. Do reinforce throughout the healing process that you want to have a happy, loving marriage.

3. Do try and go out and do fun things together to rebuild the relationship. Select activities that will enable you to enjoy each other's company, engage in laughter and get close again. Good examples would be dancing, an amusement park or a bike ride.

4. Do listen to what she has to say; show sincere interest.

5. Do be patient: changes in behavior don't necessarily happen overnight.

The Don'ts

1. Don't be negative or sarcastic. It is easy to get defensive when we are sexually frustrated, but that will not help the healing process.

2. Don't criticize your wife. You know how easy it is to be critical of small things when you are not happy, yet when you are happy you just let them go.

3. Don't threaten her with things you may regret later like opening separate checking accounts or asking the children to take sides. Be kind and supportive.

4. Don't talk to too many people about your problem. You don't want to alienate her from friends and family if things eventually work out.

5. Don't bring the children into the picture. Try and keep this as private as possible.

Over time, this may either heal the marriage or you may discover that the problem is larger than sex alone. However, that's okay. It is better to know and understand than to be left in the dark and be forever miserable. I was in an unhappy marriage for over two decades and wish that I understood these things when I was younger. It would have helped in fixing the problems or in realizing that the marriage was doomed for failure, which would have ultimately reduced my number of unhappy years.

Please, don't feel like you are unique and the only guy experiencing these problems. The divorce rate is around 50%, and even higher in some parts of the country. You are not alone! It is a major problem in our society. But the good news is that for the time being, you may have regained some of your power. It's time to be the man in your marriage for the sake of both you and your wife. Stay with me as the best is yet to come.

SEVEN

TAKE ACTION... GET IT DONE NOW!

THE SCHLOSS LEAD IN

1. *Using fear to your advantage*
2. *No Pain, No Gain in Change*
3. *Give it your best shot*

"The first step to success is taking the first step"

We have come almost full circle. The things we have talked about may even start to seem second nature. Hopefully you are enjoying the ideas presented and are experiencing really positive results in your marriage.

It is important to realize that everyone has a different situation in their marriage. Just like snowflakes, no two are exactly alike. Some men have small hills to climb to regain love while other guys may have huge mountains to transcend in their marriages. But no matter your current situation and state of affairs, the same principles apply. It is just like learning to ride a bike. Some of us go through training wheels faster than others, but eventually we all figure out how to balance and enjoy the ride.

Have you ever heard Virgil's quote, "Love Conquers All"? For the context of *The Man's Secret*, this means that if you and your wife have a *happy and sexy marriage*, you can overcome most of life's challenges and obstacles. It is a lot easier to address problems in life like money, work, family or health issues if you have a strong and loving commitment to one another.

Depending on your circumstance, you may feel like no matter what you do your wife will not respond favorably to your romantic gestures nor will she share any passion in return. My marriage was like that. When I look back, my 20-20 vision was that no matter what I did, my actions were typically perceived as being self-centered. If I only has this clarity back then, my life could have taken a *totally* different course. But you can't go back; you can only go forward!

If you have fears that your wife may reject your efforts to get back the happy and sexy, don't worry about it. What is the worst that can happen, that things will continue to be exactly the same as they are now? Big deal! Change is never easy, but the ideas presented in *The Man's Secret* are designed to be fun and derive immediate and positive results. At some point you have to try and take back the power in your marriage, establish yourself as the man, and show your wife that you want to have love and excitement like before!

For me, intimacy in a marriage is like air and water: it is essential to life. The marriage can't survive without it, and I am not just referring to sex. All of the components are critical for a marriage to be sexy and prosper.

LOOKING FEAR
IN THE EYE

A friend of mine Jeff married his wife Donna about fifteen years ago. Over time Donna became very controlling and opinionated in the marriage.

She was never happy with the money that Jeff earned or the material things that they couldn't afford in their lives. All of her friends had bigger homes and newer cars. As a result of her feeling inferior to her female friends, she took her anger out on Jeff and denied him the love and affection he felt he deserved in his life. It got to the point where Jeff didn't know what to do anymore: he was afraid to confront his wife about the problems in their relationship for fear of being berated by her.

Then one day he opened up to me about his circumstance, and we talked about how he had reached a crossroad in his marriage. He said that as much as he hated Donna today, he still felt some love for her. He also really didn't want to get a divorce, so Jeff made the decision to confront his fear of Donna's wrath. When she got mad at him, he stood up to her and told her very calmly that he would like them to address their problems. He spoke very lovingly to her, never raising his voice or allowing her to anger him. He was kind of like the Gandhi of marriage confrontation, continually reinforcing that he loved her, didn't want to argue and wanted to work things out. After a short period of time, they were able to have civil discussions again, review their marriage situation, and appreciate what they had instead of what they didn't have. This is when the A-List and 101 Ways really paid off, as they were able to start having a loving marriage again.

One of my favorite sayings is "Fear will freeze you". Fear is one of the worst emotions to overcome because it will keep you from confronting problems, trying new things and moving forward in life. Do you remember that famous quote from Franklin D. Roosevelt, "There is nothing to fear but fear itself"? Every great man that accomplishes anything in life had to look fear in the face at one point and break through the wall of uncertainty.

NO PAIN, NO GAIN IN CHANGE

Change typically comes with a cost.

Right now you are probably experiencing the pain of your current situation. You may be affected both physically and psychologically. As I mentioned earlier, I thought I was having a heart attack due to all the stress of my marriage. But now I am happy again, and I realize I had to experience that pain in order to turn my life around. I actually now feel that all of my problems happened for a reason. You can realize that too! It may not be easy to get your wife to recognize that you are sincere in wanting a happy marriage.

That is okay. Slow and easy is the way to go!

When the work day is over, do you dread coming home? Do you get a loving welcome when you walk in the house or just the opposite? After dinner, are you happy to do the dishes instead of sitting with your wife? When you walk down the street with your wife, do you not even attempt to hold hands? When you go out to dinner together, are you at a loss for conversation? When it is bed time, do you let your wife go to bed first, as you want to avoid another night of sexual frustration? If so, don't worry because you are not alone!

All of these situations didn't evolve overnight. They are the result of years of not addressing romance and intimacy in your marriage—years of not giving your wife what she needs so that she could feel loving and intimate toward you. But, now is the time to reverse the trend. Rome wasn't built in a day and neither will the renewal of your marriage. However, it is possible to regain your stature as the man in the marriage and once again sweep your wife off her feet.

Give It Your
Best Shot!

Out of all the women in the world you have met, you selected your wife for a reason. When you first met, you had great chemistry and love for each other. Yet over time the love has dissipated. You see, life is not fixed in time. It is constantly changing and moving forward. It is being aware of the changes and working together that make for a loving marriage. Some people can handle change better than others. Give it your best shot! Use all the resources and energy to make your marriage the best it can be every day. *Make a vow that your marriage is the most important thing in your life!* Make it a priority above work and other things. Decide on a course of action, and follow it!

Refer to the lists and exercises included in *The Man's Secret* to reactivate your marriage. Select a few things per week out of the "101 Ways" to re-engage with your wife. Go over the A-List to see which emotions your wife needs, and notice how she responds to your attention. Take the time to think about how you can productively use just 10 minutes per day to make your wife feel special and loved. These things, once you start, should really be a lot of fun to incorporate into your daily life. Once your wife starts to respond positively, the results will escalate exponentially.

I have even prepared some useful pages in the back of this book to help you incorporate The 1% Rule into your daily life. Since a new, learned behavior takes three weeks to become habit, I provide a daily calendar for you to plot your ideas and keep you on track for success. I call it "The Schloss 21 Day Action Plan".

To give you an idea of the power of the concepts, I shared sections of the book with other men before going to press. I sent Julian, a former work colleague, the "101 Ways" list and here is his email reply:

"I was speaking with my cousin Grant last week—a doctor and the very definition of anti-romantic—when he mentioned that his wife of thirty years had asked him to join her in dancing lessons. He was completely against it and thought it was a ridiculous idea. I immediately reached for your '101 Ways' and started reading some of them to him randomly. He was at first dismissive, saying 'That just sounds like common sense', until I read #3 (i.e. the seat belt move) and #98 (i.e. bucket list). He's tried the seat belt move and his wife LOVED it!

To my utter shock he's even agreed to the dancing lessons, an item on his wife's bucket list, which I *never* thought he'd do. I actually said to him I'd pay money to see that!"

After demonstrating your acts of affection for a few days, note how your wife reacts or responds to you. Your wife will probably be shocked at first, wouldn't you? When she asks you why you are behaving this way, tell her how much you love her and that you want to have a wonderful relationship like the day you married her. Then see if your wife starts to act more loving toward you. Go for a walk, and see how she responds to you holding her hand. Go to a movie, and see if she snuggles up close to you and puts her head on your shoulder again. Go to bed at the same time, and see if she is more receptive to your hugs and affection. Whatever happens, remember to reinforce your actions by telling her that you love her.

Just take it slow at first so as to show your wife that you are doing these things to refresh the relationship—not just for sex. Taking it slow will also reduce your chance of rejection, which you could incorrectly perceive as a setback. Don't expect crazy, wild sex after just two days. Stick with it, and in a short matter of time you will get what you want out of the marriage too. The key is being selfless and focusing on making your wife happy!

Have you heard the saying ...."I know if mama ain't happy, ain't nobody happy" (Jeff Foxworthy)? This is pretty true. Your wife can make everyone's life at home happy or miserable. By concentrating on your wife first and foremost, you will give her what she needs in the relationship in order to love you and the rest of the family.

I was talking to an industry colleague, Allen, at a conference recently and we got to talking about his family and young children. Being who I am, I asked if work and children had impacted his marriage, to which he smiled and said that "it is a challenge". Allen proceeded to tell me that he loves his wife but expressed how he wishes things were better. To which of course I had to mention that I was writing *The Man's Secret*. You should have seen his eyes light up. First, he was wondering how a fellow businessman could write a book on this topic. He knew I was divorced and I explained how much I had learned through the process. I also shared that I was passionate about helping other men.

Then I told Allen about the "101 Ways" list, to

which he immediately asked if I could share some of it. When I arrived home, I had an email waiting for me stating how much he enjoyed talking to me and that "I've got an awesome wife who I want to make sure she always knows how much I love her." This really was so nice to hear! Then he asked me again if I could share some of my "secret list". I sent a portion of the list back his way on a Friday and come Monday morning, this is what I received: "I did number 7 this weekend! (where you sit next to your wife at dinner instead of across from her). Great stuff. Thank you for the inspiration!"

You see, most of the time it is just doing the basics that is most important. Allen took his wife out for a nice dinner, but this time he made a point of sitting next to her instead of across the table. No added expense, he just enhanced the experience by making the meal more intimate and romantic. This is in no way knocking Allen. But if he can do it, you can too!

I have seen many people go through years of counseling and still not remedy their marital situation. Open communication is the first step followed by acknowledging what each person needs from the other in the marriage. Taking action and being selfless to the other person is the final step. It doesn't have to be that complicated nor does it have to take much time to get back on track.

I wish there was something like *The Man's Secret* when I was married years ago. Unfortunately, a man talking to other men about their relationships and marriage was not as common or open. But today, with the advent of the internet, men are searching more for ways to have a successful relationship.

It is really easy to get caught up in the day-to-day routine and not pay attention to the things that both the husband and wife need from each other. The quickest and easiest way to make things better is to set a game plan then assign dates and times to hold you accountable. Once you start to do things, and you see success, these new behaviors will become habit. But for now, you have to take the extra step and set a course of action. And the best way to do that is not by thinking about it in your head. Rather, it is writing things down and then doing them. Have you ever had a great idea and then said that you would remember it later…and you didn't? Use the back note pages of The Man's Secret to jot down random thoughts of things you can do that will engage and excite your wife. Come up with a system so that you don't lose these great ideas. If you don't have the book with you, send yourself an email to a personal email address that you can look at later and add to your list.

For example, let's say that your wife hinted that she would really like to go to a play? And right when she said that, you thought that it would be a great surprise to actually do it. Then as the day wore on, you forgot! But what if, as soon as you think it, you sent yourself a reminder, say via email, to buy the tickets? As soon as you see that reminder, select a convenient evening where you know you both are free and the children can be taken care of, and you buy the tickets. Now that is taking action! And how do you think your wife will react when you initiate something that she would really like to do?

Magic!

DON'T NEGLECT YOU!

THE SCHLOSS LEAD IN

1. *Make taking care of yourself a priority.*
2. *What are your passions?*
3. *Create your own Top 10 List*

"If we don't take care of ourselves, we won't be around to take care of others"

Now that we have focused on getting your sexy back by understanding the needs of your wife and the many ways to keep the "sexy" alive, let's take a moment to focus on who really counts the most in this book— YOU!

As much as we are responsible for being *the man* in the relationship and being sure that everyone is well cared for, let's not forget that we also have our own needs. Having them met is important to being happy and healthy. If we don't take care of ourselves, then we won't be around to take care of those that depend on us. Being selfless is virtuous, but it can also be harmful to our own constitution. We need to be sure that we live well-rounded lives that give us a sense of accomplishment, enjoyment and pleasure.

Statistics focusing on longevity show that married men live longer than single men, but living longer doesn't necessarily mean that married men are happier! One of the reasons that married men live longer may be due to a healthier lifestyle, as women typically cook well-rounded meals and eat more fruits and vegetables. Married men are also less likely to engage in unhealthy activities like smoking cigarettes and drinking alcohol.

But many married men also typically live more subservient lives. They work hard to help support the family and to ensure that their wife is happy and has the material things she desires in life. Just recently I was getting out of the subway in New York City and saw a middle-aged couple on the street. They were having an emotional discussion, and I overheard the man telling the woman, whom I believe was his wife, "I would buy you all the things you want if I had the money to do it." She was crying, and he was holding her hand. You could feel the love that they shared as a couple. Men are often so focused on keeping their wives happy that they don't think about taking care of themselves and enjoying their *own* lives. This typically starts right after marriage and perpetuates itself over the years. The man's day to day goal is focused on keeping peace in the relationship and getting laid on occasion.

The other reason that married men may live longer than those who are single is that divorce is one of the most stressful situations one can experience in life. For those that go through divorce, the husband and wife usually start the process somewhat amicably because they want to be fair to each other. But as the process evolves, greed sets in and it turns into a bloody battlefield over money and assets. The person you once loved now hates you with a vengeance. When I was going through my two year divorce, I developed chest pain that I thought was related to heart disease. It bothered me so much that I even went to see a cardiologist. Fortunately it ended up being stress related and not a heart attack. But this is an example of what the stress of divorce can do to your body.

As much as we want to make our wives happy, we owe it to ourselves to live happy, fulfilling lives too. If we don't, our own lives may be cut short. Then, we wouldn't be around to give our wives what they need. In many marriages, I see the women active with social activities like book clubs, yoga, lunches, etc. But most guys just go to work, return straight home, have dinner, sit on the couch, watch some TV and then go to bed. Married men don't typically have the social structure to help them navigate the emotional aspects of life. They also don't take the time to exercise and stay in shape.

WHAT ARE
YOUR PASSIONS?

To feel fulfilled and happy in life, we all need to have passions that give us identity, confidence and a sense of fulfillment other than through work. Your wife may not even know your hidden desires regarding living life to the fullest. Is she aware that you would love to learn photography, join a bowling league, or study a foreign language before visiting a faraway land? We are so busy working and being selfless for the good of the family that we neglect ourselves. This neglect impacts our health.

What things would you like to do in your life that would make you feel fulfilled and happy? You may have suppressed these thoughts for so long that it would be difficult to list even three.

One of the things I do is play tennis a few times a week. It is great not only from an exercise perspective, but it also allows me to socialize with other men. Playing tennis clears the mind for a few hours, provides stress relief from the pressures of home and work, and gives me a sense of accomplishment. Even if I lose the game, I win!

My loving girlfriend and I enjoy traveling, so we take day trips into New York City often and visit other cities (domestic and foreign) a few times a year. I also engage in two of my other passions by writing books and being a part-time disk jockey at a college radio station.

I bet that if your wife knew of your passions and desires that she would be happy to help you achieve them. If you are giving her the opportunity to enjoy her life, she should certainly give you the encouragement and opportunity to do the same.

But men can become so selfless in marriage that we focus all of our energies on providing for the woman and children at the expense of our own desires. When was the last time you spent some money on yourself? During my marriage I rarely bought myself new clothes, but my wife and kids were always fashion icons. From my experience, it is a big mistake to not stop and smell the roses.

I have a friend who goes hunting with his father and friends every fall. His wife, on the other hand, goes away for a girl's week with her mom, aunts, sisters and female friends every January. The couple supports each other to enjoy life and their individual passions. Think they have a good marriage? Taking care of yourself should also include activities that build a stronger bond between you and your wife. There is nothing better for rekindling the flame of romance than spending fun, quality time together.

OVER 90 AND STILL ROCKIN'!

I bet that men would live as long as their wives if they took care of their own physical and emotional needs. My parents, despite being 90 and 94 years old, are still rockin' together. My father Mort, the elder statesman, played tennis until he was 88. He still goes to the exercise room and rides a bike for 30 minutes every day. My mother Myra watches his diet like a hawk (she rarely lets him eat hot dogs, so I always take him for one when I visit Chicago) and supports his weekly activities with the guys. On Mondays, Mort goes to a lecture at the senior center. He finds the presentations interesting and they stimulate his mind. After the lecture, the men go out to lunch to socialize before heading back home. On Thursdays, Dad has lunch with another group of men where he is by far the oldest of the bunch. These activities are what I call healthy living and why I believe my parents are one of the few couples still intact among their peers. I must add that my mother probably has a hidden agenda in encouraging all of my dad's activities: it gets him out of the house twice a week so that she can have the ladies over to play cards and have lunch!

My father's only regret is that he didn't enjoy these types of activities when he was younger. He was so focused on providing for the family and being selfless that he never took the time to enjoy himself. Thankfully my mother recognized this during their marriage. I give her a lot of credit for the longevity, health and happiness of my father.

Your wife should give you similar support and encouragement to stimulate both your body and mind. She should want to keep you around for a long time, as growing old alone is not a lot of fun. My parents started to see some of their male friends die when they were in their sixties, so this was a wakeup call for my mother. She realized this could happen to my father too if he wasn't both physically and emotionally healthy. This is when she encouraged Dad to take up activities. He really didn't start playing tennis regularly until he retired in his sixties!

If your wife gives you any grief for your hobbies or interests, tell her that you want to do more with your life than just work for a living. Life is not like vacation days at work that you can accumulate and use at a later time. When you die, it is game over!

When my life ends, I want to feel that I did more than just make money and support a family. I have chosen to enjoy life, share passions with other people and positively influence the lives of others.

YOUR TOP TEN LIST

Seize the moment. Write a list of things you want to do in your life. Climb that mountain, visit that foreign land, learn that hobby or just make plans to get together with the guys once a week. It is never too late to make your life as fulfilling as you want.

To get your creative juices flowing, below are some ideas I have heard from other men regarding things they want to achieve in their lives. See if any of these resonate with you or if they help in creating your own list:

1. See a game at each professional baseball park.

2. Run a marathon in every state.

3. Walk the Great Wall of China.

4. Play golf at the top 10 public courses.

5. Learn how to be a chef.

6. Climb a mountain.

7. Go helicopter skiing in Utah.

8. Hike through the Grand Canyon.

9. Learn a musical instrument or foreign language.

10. Write a book.

In the last pages of this book, I have given you space to list your own Top Ten List. Writing down your ideas is the first step to action. I have also provided a column to list the date you would like to accomplish each item on the list. Refer to it often, and set a plan to achieve them. Even if you only accomplish a few items on your list, wouldn't that still be awesome! Most people say that they will do things, but they never make it happen. By writing your own list and setting dates, you are now on the way to making yourself accountable for achieving your goals.

THE MAN'S SECRET HAPPY LIST...
WHAT DO YOU WANT *FROM* YOUR WIFE?

1. *Recognizing that the man needs to be happy in the marriage too*
2. *What's your Happy List?*
3. *Reinforcing your wife's positive behavior*

"If you treated each other like when you were dating, you would have a lot sexier marriage today!"

We have spent a great deal of the book focusing on being somewhat selfless and making your wife happy. The premise is that if your wife is happy, you will be happy too. The result will be a more loving, affectionate marriage.

But what exactly are you looking for out of your marriage? Men are truly pretty simple creatures. We only need a few material and emotional things to feel really good about our lives. What things could your wife do for you that would make you really happy? Based on my experience, women don't realize that men also need the same recognition or compliments we garnish on them.

As good as your wife feels when you tell her how beautiful or wonderful she is, do you receive unsolicited compliments back? It is just not as special when you first tell your wife that she is beautiful and then in response she tells you that you are handsome as well. Or what if your wife tells you that she loves you only after you say it to her first? I don't know about you, but I feel really good about myself when I am told, totally unsolicited, that I am a great lover or an appreciated provider! Is this something that would make you feel really special to hear from your wife too?

I have been told by some men that they really don't care if they are paid compliments by their wives. It is more important to them to receive support for the things that they like to do. They don't want to feel guilty for hanging out with the guys, going biking, playing golf or any other activity. They just want their wives to support them and not make them feel wrong for doing what they enjoy.

I have created a very short exercise to help you prioritize both what you want and what you are already getting from your marriage.

Listed below are a number of behaviors. For each behavior, indicate how important that particular behavior is to your marriage. Use a scale of 1 to 10, with 10 being the highest. In the last column, indicate if your wife is or is not providing or allowing for that particular behavior. Please take your time, and be totally honest with yourself. If there are some behaviors that I did not include that are important to you, go ahead and list them at the end of the list.

THE MAN'S SECRET HAPPY LIST

Behavior	Score (1-10)	Getting It?
▪ I want sex on a weekly basis	═══	═══

- I want to hear that I am a good lover   ===   ===
- I want open communication   ===   ===
- I want to hear that I am handsome   ===   ===
- I want to hear that I am a good husband   ===   ===
- I want to hear that I am a good father   ===   ===
- I want to hear that I am a good provider   ===   ===
- I want to hear that my wife loves me   ===   ===
- I want to feel appreciated   ===   ===
- I want to minimize conflicts and arguments   ===   ===
- I want my wife to support my hobbies and interests   ===   ===
- I want my wife to support my male friendships   ===   ===
- I want my wife to support my exercise time   ===   ===
- I want time alone with my wife   ===   ===
- I want to spend time with my parents and siblings   ===   ===

- I want my wife to be more adventurous in bed ═══ ═══
- I want my wife to give me a backrub or caress me on occasion ═══ ═══
- I want my wife to not guilt me into things ═══ ═══
- I want my wife to not overspend ═══ ═══
- I want my wife to respect my alone time ═══ ═══
- I want my wife to sometimes put me before her family ═══ ═══

Other behaviors not listed:

_____

_____

_____

Take the behaviors where you answered "NO" and figure out which three have the highest scores. This is your "**Want List**".

Next, take the three behaviors where you

answered "YES" and figure out which three have the highest scores. This is your "**Appreciation List**".

THE WANT LIST

The "Want List" is comprised of three things to tell your wife you would like to receive from her in the marriage. As you are going out of your way to give her what she needs, why not lovingly tell her the things that are important for you to receive back? For example, you could explain to your wife that it would be really nice to hear that she thinks you handsome or a good lover. You could also explain that you like hearing the time you spend in the gym is noticeable and she finds you very sexy.

Over time, you can expand the "Want List" to include more behaviors, but it is best to start out with just a few and see how your wife responds to your requests for acknowledgement.

I met a woman recently and asked her if she thought she knew what makes her husband happy. She paused, and then said, "He wants to feel appreciated." I asked her what else makes him happy, and she responded, "He really likes it when I rub his back and hug him." I followed this up by asking if he lets her know that he likes these things, to which she stated, "Yes, he definitely lets me know how much he enjoys me doing these things for him."

This story, from my experience, is not the norm. I don't think most men let their wives know what makes them happy, except maybe with sex. Since communication is the key to a successful marriage, would you feel comfortable telling your wife what makes you happy? At first it may feel a little awkward, but another one of my favorite sayings in life is "If you don't ask, you don't get." Don't you think your wife would love to know what's on your "Want List"? Hasn't your wife asked you about your fantasies or dreams in the past?

Seize the opportunity and tell your wife what you want! How are wives supposed to provide support if husbands don't let them know what they want? Some people are intuitive when giving compliments and recognizing other people's wants. For others, they need to learn this or get reminders. It doesn't mean your wife thinks poorly of you or your actions if she doesn't currently give compliments. It just means that you need to let her know how you feel and what is important to you. Once you do and she sees the smiles on your face, as well as the positive reinforcement she receives back, it will become second nature over time. *This* is what makes for a happy couple!

THE APPRECIATION LIST

The "Appreciation List" is made up of the top three things your wife gives you in the marriage. You need to tell her how much you appreciate receiving these specific things from her. For example, if your wife encourages you to go fishing once a month, you should let her know how much you appreciate her support and the extra work she has to do when you are away for a weekend, not to mention dealing with all the dirty, smelly clothes you bring back!

A college friend, Harold, and I reacquainted at an event in New York City. He was married and had a young child. Harold was telling me that as soon as his wife became pregnant, all of the focus was on her. Having a baby was certainly a big deal, but his wife rarely ever paid much attention to Harold— even after the baby was born. All of their conversations and activities were focused on her pregnancy and raising the baby.

Needless to say, Harold was not feeling appreciated for everything he did for the family. He began to feel that his wife perceived him solely as the bread winner and sperm donor. Once Harold realized why he felt so minimized in the marriage, he gently talked to his wife about his needs. At first she was defensive, but Harold said that for him to be happy in the marriage he needed some appreciation for everything he does. This was a wake-up call for his wife. She started to let Harold know what a wonderful husband, father and provider he has been throughout the years.

This is a really good exercise to get you thinking about what you would like out of your marriage and to encourage you to take proactive steps toward reinforcing or attaining them. It is so easy to get wrapped up with work and raising a family that you neglect thinking about what would make you happy. This is your chance to prioritize your life and make your marriage a win-win scenario. By this I mean you want to give your wife the things that will make her happy, but you also want to feel like you are getting pleasure from the marriage in return.

If for some reason you are not receiving the accolades that you want from your wife, then you may want to consider some of the strategies in the "Four Strategies to Get Sex Back in Your Marriage" chapter. Think about it: In a sexy marriage, what actions can you take to get your wife to reciprocate? If you tell her what would make you happy and she doesn't comply, what can you do?

If it was me, I would initially stop giving her the compliments or positive reinforcement that she has been receiving from me. Observe how long it takes for her to notice and for her to subsequently react. I bet she will quickly miss all the loving things that you say to her. When she notices it, ask her if she misses all the attention that you were giving her before. If she says yes, tell her why you stopped. Marriage is a two-way street, and sometimes you should expect to receive as well as give. See if that kick starts a positive behavior!

IN CLOSING...
a note from Steve

> *"Give 10 minutes a day and get a lifetime of Happy and Sexy"*

"If I only knew then what I know now..." How often have you said this phrase to yourself? For me, if I added the words "it may have saved my marriage," it would be even more profound.

Have you thought of what this phrase means? It means that you have grown wiser over the years due to your life experiences. It also means that you have been smart enough to recognize the mistakes you made in the past and apply those to your life today.

When I set out to write *The Man's Secret*, my goal was to share with married men the lessons I learned over the past twenty-five plus years of my life. I recognized from talking to other men that the emotions and circumstances I experienced in marriage were not unique, but actually quite common. Most of us will reach a point where we realize that we need to stop going around in circles and look for some marital advice from a self-acknowledged, middle-aged relationship guru!

If by chance you are a woman reading *The Man's Secret*, I commend you for your curiosity to learn the man's perspective and hope that you lovingly share this information with your husband as a map to a wonderful, restored marriage.

From day one I said that if I was able to help just one man with his marriage, then it would be worth all the effort. You see, writing *The Man's Secret* has also benefited me personally. It helped me gain clarity in my own life, heal from my divorce, establish a new loving relationship and achieve renewed confidence in myself. It was one of the best, most personally rewarding experiences of my life…probably second only to having children.

I continue to learn about relationships every day. Every person I talk to shares new insights that allow me to create new theories and test new solutions to make relationships as beautiful and fulfilling as possible. You see, I don't know everything and for every question I answer, ten more come to mind. That is what makes being a student of life and relationships so much fun! And it also gives me ideas for future books and classes.

Not only was my twenty-four year marriage troublesome, my girlfriend and I have had our good and bad days too. There are always bumps in the road, some of which we have control over and others not. But the two things that hold us together are communication and being selfless to each other. We refuse to let problems go for very long without talking about them. In fact, I have a rule that we never go to sleep without talking about things bothering us. My other rule is that we don't have negative discussions via email or text.

I have a friend Benny that I hadn't seen in about three years, before I met my girlfriend. I ran into him recently on the train and he asked me if I was still on the dating scene, as he jokingly said that he wanted to "live vicariously" through me. I told Benny that I had a girlfriend now and that the way he should be living vicariously is through my wonderfully loving and affectionate relationship. Most married men dream of being single again and dating lots of women. But what I found from my years of dating, prior to meeting my girlfriend, is that dating can be very lonely and shallow. Sure it was fun to "experience" new women, but I realized that the glass was only half full without the love. This wouldn't have resonated when I was unhappily married, but now I realize that there is nothing better than a loving partnership.

So I make this pledge to you, my reader.

Try the ideas and solutions that I share. Have a positive attitude that you can have a wonderful, loving marriage. Let your wife know that she is the most important thing in your life. Put her first and wait for the magic to happen. It will be like spring time again in your marriage, your relationship abloom with new growth and fresh fruits to bear.

Give it your best shot! Be a devoted husband. Now is the time to let go of the past and start fresh. Forget about all the "shoulda, coulda, wouldas" that happened yesterday. It doesn't matter anymore. Take your wife in your arms and let her know that you love her and want to have a wonderful marriage. Then follow through with sincere actions that are consistent with your pledge. You will find that there really isn't anything better than a supportive, loving relationship.

If you have found my book beneficial to your marriage, please tell a friend so that they can share equally in the joy of a wonderful relationship. And let the rest of the world know how the book has improved your life by writing a review on Amazon.com. You can also email me at steve@mantomantalks.com to keep me posted on your progress.

Writing this, my first book, has been a labor of love. I hope that it helps in elevating romance and passion in your life. I hope that it opens the channels of communication to avoid divorce. And last, I hope your wife thinks that you are the best thing that ever happened to her.

Steve

ACKNOWLEDGEMENTS

Anthea Margot—My love and my most ardent supporter. Your ever expanding talents as designer of my wonderful logo and book interior, brilliant cartoonist and exceptional photographer far exceeded all expectations. It was so much fun collaborating with you. Thank you Sweetie!

Tim Bryant—Thank you for working with me in the early stages of the project and believing in the concept.

Barbara Barnes—A big thank you for loving the idea from the start and how you kept telling me, "You have to do it!"

William Shane Tucker—Thank you for professionalism and concise editing, and for keeping it real.

Kathi Dunn—Thank you for designing my beautiful cover that met the goal of being attractive to both men and women alike.

John Kremer—Thank you for your numerous contributions in creating a wonderful book title and back cover copy.

Jeff Ourvan—Thank you for your professional insights and encouragement.

All the other people who shared words of encouragement throughout the process: Mark Majors, Justin Nathan, Jeremy Girrbach, James McKeever, Debbie Schwartz, Clint Horner and Jill Baskind

WORK WITH STEVE

Why not have the best marriage you can have today?

If your marriage is in a state of emergency or if it just needs a tune-up, I can help!

I offer One-on-One coaching and mentoring to reactivate the "happy and *sexy*" in your marriage or relationship. And you will see results literally overnight.

We will work together to understand what your wife needs from you today so that she will want to give you what you need in return. Fun exercises and discussions reveal the challenges in your marriage plus we'll develop actionable solutions that you can deploy right now. You won't believe the changes you see in your wife after just one session!

Why work with a relationship coach? Because a coach can help you uncover the issues in your marriage and provide accountability. It is so easy to say you are going to do something but never do it. Working with a coach is that important first step to taking action and making it happen.

Your marriage should be the most important thing in your life. Nothing will give you a better return on investment than focusing on having a wonderful, loving relationship.

To start the process, visit:
 www.mantomantalks.com and click on the "Work With Steve" button.

You can also email me at:
steve@mantomantalks.com to learn more.

Steve

THE A-LIST EXERCISE
REFERRING TO CHAPTER 3

Thinking back to the A-List, what have you discovered that your wife needs from you? Does she need more Acceptance, Admiration, Adoration or Appreciation?

Let's jot down some ways of communicating with your wife that address her emotional needs. Then notice her reactions and note which categories get the most favorable response. For today, these are the areas where she needs the most positive acknowledgement.

Just note that the category that needs the most attention today may be different tomorrow or next month. You know how they say that the three most important things in buying real estate are location, location, and location. Well for your marriage, they are reevaluate, reevaluate and reevaluate.

APPRECIATION

List three things here where you can show your wife how much she is appreciated. Some examples would be: I want to tell my wife more about how much I appreciate her, such as raising the kids and taking care of the house.

1.

2.

3.

ADORATION

List three things here where you can show your wife how much you adore her. Examples are: I want to tell my wife how much I love her smile, how happy she makes me or how I find her legs so sexy when she wears a skirt.

1.

2.

3.

ACCEPTANCE

Let's list three things here where you can show your wife that she is accepted for exactly who she is and criticize her less. Some examples would be: I want to overlook the small things, like how she forgets to put the top back on the toothpaste or bring in the garbage cans. Instead I will accept this behavior and just do it for her with a big smile on my face.

1.

2.

3.

ADMIRATION

List three things that you admire about your wife that she will be really happy to hear from you. For example: I want to let my wife know wonderful she is being active with community activities, caring for her aging parents or raising the children.

1.

2.

3.

Are you starting to see patterns here of how you need to communicate with your wife so that she thinks you are wonderful and caring?

After addressing her A-List needs for just a day or two, you should expect to see a major change in how your wife interacts with you. You will once again be the loving, caring, compassionate husband that she married and she will show you love in return.

TAKE ACTION
USING THE 1% RULE:
"The Schloss 21 Day Action Plan"

5 IDEAS A DAY TO
ENGAGE WITH MY WIFE AND
MAKE HER FEEL SPECIAL

Let's take a few minutes to think about "The 1% Rule" and how you can use it today!

As you will recall, we talked about using *less than 10 minutes a day* to engage with your wife. I have provided space for you to fill in five of your own ideas for 21 days, as this is an exercise that will help you form a healthy new habit. And remember it is not just the amount of time you dedicate to this; it is also the number of times you make your wife feel loved throughout the day.

Check out these short and easy examples of things you can do to make your wife feel special. After doing this for just one day, you will see a big difference in how your wife greets you after work.

Note how she is now more responsive to you in your renewed role of her "leading-man".

And don't stop now, prepare for tomorrow by creating a new list of 5 ideas to keep the fire burning.

To keep this really fresh, try to do at least one new thing every day that you had not done prior. Make it fun and see how much you can surprise your wife!

SAMPLE IDEAS:

- Buy a rose and leave it on her windshield.

- Before leaving for work, make a point of giving her a hug and a compliment, like telling her how beautiful she is or how much you love her.

- Text her when you get to work and let her know you wish you could be spending the day with her.

- Call her in the afternoon and see how her day is going. Remember to ask her about something that she had planned, like a presentation at work or lunch with a friend.

Then tell her that you love her at the end of the call.

- Call her before heading home and ask if there is anything you can do or pick up...then tell her you can't wait to give her a big hug when you walk in the door.

- After dinner, ask your wife to take a walk with you around the neighborhood...and don't forget to hold her hand!

- When you sit on the couch with her in the evening, give her a shoulder massage and see how she reacts.

- And don't forget the weekend where you can make her breakfast in bed, go out to lunch or dinner, see a movie, text her sweet things, go dancing, go biking or any variety of other activities where you can have fun, laugh and be close.

"THE SCHLOSS 21 DAY ACTION PLAN"

MY 5 IDEAS FOR DAY 1 OF WEEK 1

1.

2.

3.

4.

5.

MY 5 IDEAS FOR DAY 2:

1.

2.

3.

4.

5.

MY 5 IDEAS FOR DAY 3:

1.

2.

3.

4.

5.

MY 5 IDEAS FOR DAY 4:

1.

2.

3.

4.

5.

MY 5 IDEAS FOR DAY **5**:

1.

2.

3.

4.

5.

MY 5 IDEAS FOR DAY **6**:

1.

2.

3.

4.

5.

MY 5 IDEAS FOR DAY 7

1.

2.

3.

4.

5.

MY 5 IDEAS FOR DAY 1 OF WEEK 2:

1.

2.

3.

4.

5.

MY 5 IDEAS FOR DAY 2 OF WEEK 2:

1.

2.

3.

4.

5.

MY 5 IDEAS FOR DAY 3 OF WEEK 2:

1.

2.

3.

4.

5.

MY 5 IDEAS FOR DAY 4 OF WEEK 2:

1.

2.

3.

4.

5.

MY 5 IDEAS FOR DAY 5 OF WEEK 2:

1.

2.

3.

4.

5.

MY 5 IDEAS FOR DAY **6** OF WEEK 2:

1.

2.

3.

4.

5.

MY 5 IDEAS FOR DAY **7** OF WEEK 2:

1.

2.

3.

4.

5.

MY 5 IDEAS FOR DAY **1** OF WEEK 3:

1.

2.

3.

4.

5.

MY 5 IDEAS FOR DAY **2** OF WEEK 3:

1.

2.

3.

4.

5.

MY 5 IDEAS FOR DAY **3** OF WEEK 3:

1.

2.

3.

4.

5.

MY 5 IDEAS FOR DAY **4** OF WEEK 3:

1.

2.

3.

4.

5.

MY 5 IDEAS FOR DAY **5** OF WEEK 3:

1.

2.

3.

4.

5.

MY 5 IDEAS FOR DAY 6 OF WEEK 3:

1.

2.

3.

4.

5.

MY 5 IDEAS FOR DAY 7 OF WEEK 3:

1.

2.

3.

4.

5.

THE MAN'S SECRET
TOP 10 LIST OF
THINGS TO ACHIEVE IN LIFE:

What are the top ten things you want to do during your life? Write them down here and include a goal date for completing them as well as when they are actually completed. Refer to the list often for a reminder, update and to check off. You can do anything you want in life; you just have to plan and set goals. It may mean saving $10 per week for five years to accumulate enough money to go surfing in Hawaii, but you can do it. When you do, you will be so proud of how you accomplished your goal. After you've done it once, doing the next thing will be even easier!

Don't forget to let me know about your progress by emailing me at Steve@mantomantalks.com.

<u>My Top Ten List:</u>   <u>Goal Date</u>   <u>Finish Date</u>

1.

2.

3.

4.

5.

6.

7.

8.

9.

10.

THE MAN'S SECRET NOTES

_____

_____

_____

_____

_____

_____

_____

_____

_____

_____

_____

_____

_____

_____

_____

_____

_____

_____

_____

_____

_____

_____

_____

_____

_____

_____

_____

_____

_____

www.ingramcontent.com/pod-product-compliance
Lightning Source LLC
Chambersburg PA
CBHW060846280326
41934CB00007B/939